Isabel Müller

Clicker Training
for Rabbits, Guinea Pigs,
and Other Small Pets

Clicker Training for Rabbits, Guinea Pigs, and Other Small Pets

CompanionHouse Books™ is an imprint of Fox Chapel Publishing Company, Inc.

Clickertraining für Kaninchen, Meerschweinchen & Co. © 2018 by Eugen Ulmer KG, Stuttgart, Germany

English edition Copyright © 2023 by Fox Chapel Publishing Company, Inc.,
903 Square Street, Mount Joy, PA 17552.

Project Team
Editors: Madeline DeLuca, Amy Deputato
Copy Editor: Colleen Dorsey
Design: Mary Ann Kahn
Translator: Ian Kahn

German Project Team
Proofreaders: Kathrin Gutmann, Heike Schmidt-Röger
Production: Katharina Merz
Cover Concept: Ruska, Martín, Associates GmbH, Berlin
Cover Design: Atelier Reichert

ISBN 978-1-62008-387-1

Library of Congress Control Number: 2020010090

We are always looking for talented authors. To submit an idea, please send a brief inquiry to acquisitions@foxchapelpublishing.com.

Note to Professional Copy Services:
The publisher grants you permission to make up to ten copies of any training log pages in this book for any customer who purchased this book and states the copies are for personal use.

Printed in China
26 25 24 23   2 4 6 8 10 9 7 5 3 1

This book has been published with the intent to provide accurate and authoritative information in regard to the subject matter within. While every precaution has been taken in the preparation of this book, the author and publisher expressly disclaim any responsibility for any errors, omissions, or adverse effects arising from the use or application of the information contained herein. The techniques and suggestions are used at the reader's discretion and are not to be considered a substitute for veterinary care. If you suspect a medical problem, consult your veterinarian.

Contents

11

23

37

45

Chapter 4

Using the Target Stick

53

Chapter 5

The Target Stick: Your Magic Wand

69

Chapter 6

Tricks with Clicks

87

Chapter 7

Click According to Plan

7

Clicking at a Glance

There are many possibilities once you have clicker trained your pet. From performing tricks to correcting bad behavior, both you and your pet can benefit from the help of a clicker.

Summary of Exercises

Exercise	Difficulty level	Suitable for	Training location	Training method
Slalom	Easy	All small pets	Outside the pen	Guide your pet to weave back and forth through a line of objects using a target stick.
Running Through a Tunnel	Easy	All small pets	Outside the pen	Guide your pet to and eventually through a small tunnel with a target stick, rewarding for success at each step.
Hiding under a Blanket	Easy	All small pets	Outside the pen	Guide your pet to an opening in a blanket for him to crawl into and eventually under, rewarding for success at each step.
Walking on a Seesaw	Easy to medium	All small pets (more difficult for larger, less agile pets like guinea pigs)	Outside the pen	Guide the pet to walk up one side and then down the other side of a seesaw using a target stick.
Turning in Circles	Easy	All small pets	Outside the pen	Encourage your pet to touch the target stick with his nose and follow it around in a circle.
Jumping Through a Hoop	Medium	Small pets who like to jump (including rabbits, degus, and chinchillas)	Outside the pen	Guide the pet to jump through a low ring or hoop using a target stick.
Overcoming the Fear of Being Touched	Depends on the severity of fear	Any small pet who is afraid of being touched	Outside the pen	You become part of the training course and guide the pet to approach you, touch you, and even climb on you using a target stick. (Use the same process to overcome fear of any objects.)
Standing Up on Hind Legs	Easy with the target stick; difficult with a cue word	All small pets (more difficult for less agile pets and those who have trouble balancing)	Outside the pen	Teach the pet to stand on his hind legs using a target stick and then progress to using a verbal cue.
Coming on Cue	Medium to difficult	All small pets who are already comfortable with people	Outside the pen	Guide the pet to come to you using a target stick along with a verbal cue. You can also use the verbal cue without the target stick whenever the pet approaches you on his own.

Clicker Training for Rabbits, Guinea Pigs, and Other Small Pets

Exercise	Difficulty level	Suitable for	Training location	Training method
Give Me Five (and Give Me Ten)	Medium	All small pets (easier to teach to rabbits and larger rodents)	Outside the pen	Guide the pet to stretch up for the target stick and touch his foot when he lifts it. You can gradually fade out the target stick and add a verbal cue if you'd like.
Playing Soccer	Easy to medium	Rabbits and larger rodents	Outside the pen	Reward the pet for touching and pushing a ball; no target stick required.
Playing Basketball	Easy to medium	Mainly rabbits	Outside the pen	Reward the pet for grabbing the ball with his teeth and then dropping it; no target stick required.
House-Training	Medium	All small pets (works especially well with rabbits)	First in the pen, then outside the pen	Encourage the pet to use a litter box; reward him when he does. If he attempts to do his business elsewhere, redirect him to the litter box.
Getting Used to Being Picked Up	Medium	All small pets who are accustomed to being touched but afraid of being picked up	In the pen and outside the pen	Work with a training assistant: one person lifts the pet, and the other rewards the pet for staying calm. Use two verbal cues, such as "up" and "down" (for putting him back down).
Getting Used to the Pet Carrier	Easy to medium	All small pets	Outside the pen, then in the carrier	Guide the pet to the carrier with the target stick. Reward him for staying calm in the carrier.
Good Behavior in the Cage	Medium	All small pets	In the cage or pen	Reward the pet for passive action, such as waiting before being fed, and ignore undesirable behavior, such as gnawing on the cage bars.
Stress-Free Nail Clipping	Medium	All small pets who do not like having their nails clipped	Outside the pen, on your lap	Introduce nail clipping in small steps; reward the pet's calm behavior during each step. It is useful to work with a training assistant.
Sitting Still for Grooming	Medium	All small pets who dislike grooming	Outside the pen, either on the trainer's lap or on the floor	Reward calm behavior during brushing, gradually increasing the length of grooming sessions.
No Unwanted Chewing	Difficult; success not guaranteed	All small pets	Outside the pen	Reinforce chewing on suitable objects, such as branches. Remove the pet from the area if he tries to chew forbidden objects, such as electrical cords.

CHAPTER 1

"Click" with Your Pet

>>

Hiding in a blanket is just one of many tricks you can teach your pet through clicker training.

Clicker Training Basics

Clicker training really started gaining popularity with pet owners around the early 1990s, but its origins go back further in the twentieth century. In 1938, behavioral scientist B.F. Skinner and his students first attempted using a reward immediately following a sound in training animals. In the years that followed, new knowledge about animals' learning behavior was applied in a variety of ways. Animals were trained for tasks like performing in commercials and on TV shows, but they were also used as tools for questionable military purposes—for example, animals were taught to trigger ignition mechanisms in weapons or to bring mines to hostile areas.

The first publications on clicker training were published in the United States in the mid-twentieth century. In the 1960s, Karen Pryor, a student of Skinner's who would become an authority on clicker training, started using clickers to train dolphins for aquarium shows. She quickly realized that this form of training helped the animals learn more effectively and with less stress than previous training methods, which used punishment for incorrect behaviors.

Thanks to this research, the relationship between humans and animals improved enormously. Animals were no longer simply trained as tools for humans, and trainers began to consider the animals' needs more and more during training. People realized that clicker training could be used as a playful pursuit to help improve animals' lives and the humans' bond with animals.

Gradually, in the early 1990s, dog trainers throughout the United States

This guinea pig is focused on a target stick, another useful tool for clicker training (see page 15).

and Europe began adopting this new method, especially for search and rescue dogs, police dogs, guide dogs, and therapy dogs. Dog owners also started using the clicker method to train their pets at home. Readers were intrigued by the mentions of clicker training in dog magazines. Since that time, clicker training has become a well-known and recognized training method for all types of pets, and it is used by professional animal trainers and enthusiastic pet owners alike.

What Does It Mean to Learn?

Each animal species has an innate pattern of behavior—movements, actions, and reactions, including noises, postures, and visually recognizable changes in attitude—that the animal displays in certain situations. In addition to genetically predisposed behaviors, learned behaviors are part of this pattern. Most living creatures are able to add new behavioral elements to their innate behavioral patterns by learning. Through learned behavior, an animal can adapt to new situations just like humans can, which increases his chances of survival.

The requirement for any type of learning is memory, which enables the storage and recall of information. We assume that nerves make new connections with each step in the learning process, which then become stored in memory. Behavioral biologists, psychologists, and other scientists have described different types of learning that have been derived from various research approaches.

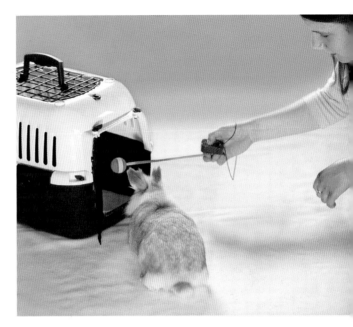

You can use clicker training to introduce your pet to his carrier.

DID YOU KNOW?

Learning Disposition

The ease with which a creature is able to learn something is its learning disposition and is determined by genetics. This is why it is easier to teach a human to run away from a snake than from a dandelion. If a rat feels sick after eating something, he can connect this feeling to the taste of the food. He cannot, however, link this feeling to the sound of a bell that rings at feeding time.

Learning with the Clicker

The basic principle of clicker training is *linking* or *associative learning*. Various external stimuli (e.g., noises) are linked to the animal's behaviors to form connections. A connection between a stimulus and the animal's reaction becomes stronger if the reaction has a positive aftereffect, e.g., it is followed by a reward.

For animals to learn quickly, this reward needs to take place as soon as possible after the reaction—almost at the same time. That is why the click sound and the reward that immediately follow the desired behavior during clicker training are so well suited to successful learning.

Animals learn behavior through trial, error, and accidental success. You can best understand this type of learning with the help of the Skinner Box, named after the

DID YOU KNOW?

Rewards = Success

Giving treats and other rewards is referred to as "positive reinforcement" because the right behavior occurs more frequently after the animal is rewarded for a few successful attempts.

famous behavioral researcher B.F. Skinner. The Skinner Box works like this: An animal (e.g., a rat) is put in a cage with an automatic feeder. The hungry animal will receive food from the feeder every time he pulls a certain lever correctly. At first, the animal's movements are random, but if he accidentally pulls the lever correctly, he is rewarded with food.

After a while, the animal will recognize the connection between the lever and the food. With repeated success, the animal creates a link between his actions and the

Food rewards, clickers, and target sticks are all the materials you need for clicker training.

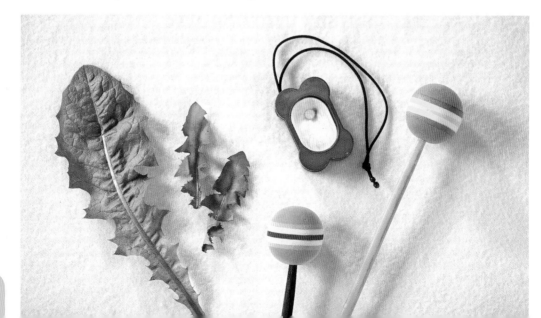

reward: the learning process is fostered by the reward. The same is true with clicker training.

Target Stick Training

As you will read in chapters 4 and 5, another great tool for clicker training is the target stick. A target stick is a stick with a ball on one end that you can use to guide your pet toward a specific goal. You will soon learn how to guide your pet with both the clicker and the target stick in order to achieve a goal or perform a trick. Your animal will soon associate both the clicker and the target stick with a reward, thus making clicker training all the more fun and easy.

Punishment Is Taboo

It should go without saying that you should never punish your pet, be it in the form of scolding, shouting, or physical punishment. Animals never act out of malice. If your pet makes a mistake during training, it is certainly not to annoy you; he probably just did not understand what you asked him to do.

Using punishment in such a situation can frighten your pet to the point that he completely refuses to work with you. If training with you becomes a scary situation for the animal, he will try to avoid it.

The effect of positive reinforcement also lasts much longer than that of negative reinforcement and is the only way for animals to learn complex tasks—this is because the connection between

Food rewards are the most effective rewards to use in clicker training.

stimulus and reaction becomes stronger if the reaction is followed by a positive reinforcer, and the connection becomes weaker if a negative aftereffect is the result.

Therefore, if you notice that your pet is not focused or is making too many mistakes, do not punish him! This is a clear sign that your little friend does not properly understand what you expect of him and therefore cannot execute the behavior correctly. Take a step back in your training plan and practice the previous step of the exercise until it is perfect—only then should you move on to the next step.

Tip

End on a High Note

Lack of concentration is sometimes a sign of lack of interest. If your pet is losing focus, end the training with an exercise that the animal particularly enjoys and try again at a later time. This way, you end the training session with a positive experience.

Clicking Consistently

You may be familiar with the frog clicker, a classic small tin toy that makes a characteristic clicking sound when you press on a metal spring. A clicker for training animals works in a similar way, except the spring is inside a small handheld box, and you press on a metal plate to hear the distinctive click.

Of course, you can use a different source of noise for clicker training, e.g., your tongue or a ballpoint pen. Both of these methods, however, have disadvantages. When you click your tongue, the sound it makes is a little different each time. This can make training confusing for the animal, at which point he may refuse to cooperate. The ballpoint pen poses a similar problem because the click of the pen is not distinct enough for the animal to consistently

recognize. Also, if you are using a ballpoint pen at times other than your training sessions, and your pet hears the click but does not get a reward, it can be very frustrating for him because he will assume that you were clicking the pen for him.

So, it certainly makes sense to buy a clicker, especially since clickers are relatively inexpensive and are available in almost every pet-supply store as well as online. Generally, these clickers are meant for training dogs, but they are just as suitable for clicker training with guinea pigs, rabbits, and other small pets.

Conditioning to the Clicker

In animal training, the animal must receive the reward as soon as possible after the desired behavior—almost simultaneously—because this is the only

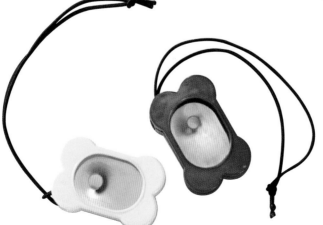

There are many different types of clickers available in pet-supply stores.

way to increase learning success. It is faster to make a quick click immediately after the desired behavior than to give a treat a few seconds later. Also, because the clicking sound is always the same, your rodent or rabbit will learn after just a few exercises that he will be rewarded immediately after the click.

A click means "Well done! A reward is coming." The clicker is therefore a bridge between the desired behavior and the reward for this behavior. The clicking sound makes it easier for the animal to understand that he has done what you want or that he has behaved correctly. Your pet will quickly learn to associate the familiar click with something positive:

Tristan the rabbit knows that the reward comes right after the click.

Adjust the Volume

Tip

For a noise-sensitive animal, use a clicker that allows you to adjust the volume of the click.

the reward. In other words, your pet will become "conditioned" to the clicker.

Using the Clicker Properly

The following steps give you an overview of how to use the clicker to accomplish a behavior:

1 Condition the animal to the clicker (see chapter 3).

2 Create a training plan for the exercise. First, identify the goal behavior and then think about how the behavior can be broken down into a series of individual movements or steps. Make note of the sequence of steps.

3 Start training by introducing the first step, clicking and rewarding immediately after each correct response. Keep practicing this step; take it slow. Once your pet has mastered the first step (it may take a few days), add the next step. Work with your animal step by step until he can perform the entire behavior. Remember that many small successes add up to the goal.

With this method, your training partner (a.k.a. your pet) will learn step by step because each small movement on the way to the final goal is individually practiced and rewarded, and it is easier to learn a sequence of small, simple steps than an entire exercise all at once. This way of teaching also makes the final behavior—the result of all the small steps put together—easier for the animal to understand and repeat.

Reinforce each individual step with the click and the subsequent reward, and only when the animal continues to perform a step correctly (even if it takes a few days of training) do you move on to the next step. Remember: small intermediate goals will give you and your pet the most success.

Because the movements that make up a behavior can be very small and happen very quickly, the clicker enables you to deliver the reinforcement immediately and accurately after each desired movement. A quick click lets the animal know that the reward will follow right away. With a little patience and practice, you will eventually be able to teach your training partner longer sequences of movements that result in more complex behaviors.

Advantages of Clicker Training

> Clicker training is based on reward, not punishment. The animal will have no negative experiences during training, so the human-animal relationship gets better and better as you train.
> To be a clicker trainer, you don't need a lot of previous knowledge. Anyone can train his or her pet by approaching training with patience, fun, and consistency.
> Clicker training is more than just teaching tricks. With the help of targeted exercises, you can resolve some behavioral problems, such as the pet scratching when you pick him up (see pages 70–71).
> Clicker training gives the animal a feeling of security. He learns that he is able to communicate with his owner and actively participate in changes in his environment. He can exercise a certain amount of control in various situations.
> Clicker training is an inexpensive training method. In addition to the clicker, you need only a target stick (see chapter 4), which you can easily make yourself.

Is Clicker Training the Key to Happiness?

At first glance, this question may seem a little confusing. Didn't I just explain in detail the positive effects that clicker training has on humans and animals? That it strengthens the human-animal relationship, prevents boredom, and can even correct minor behavioral problems?

I do not intend to refute these statements, and although clicker training is ideal for small animals, I would like to point out that, even with clicker training, you must not neglect other important areas of pet ownership. An animal who practices clicker training with his owner but is lonely for the rest of the time, has no other interaction with people or other pets, and lives in a cage that is too small will not be a happy animal no matter how much clicker training you do.

There are many ways to learn about your pet's needs and wants, and I would like to give you a brief overview of the basic rules you must follow for animal welfare. After all, if you are not fulfilling the essentials, you should first invest your time and energy in improving your animal's living conditions before you begin training.

When choosing an enclosure, the bigger, the better. Remember that your pet will spend most of his life in it. Animals in cages that are too small often suffer from excessive weight, underdeveloped muscles, and boredom. You may be able to attach a securely enclosed run-out area to your pet's cage, which will give him more room to stretch his legs and play. These come in a variety of configurations.

The animal's pen should be made of as many natural materials as possible. For example, a plastic house can be harmful if your pet decides to nibble on it. In addition, plastic enclosures often get waterlogged, which can lead to health problems. It is also nice to vary the cage setup from time to time to provide more variety.

Rabbits, guinea pigs, chinchillas, and many other small mammals naturally live in family groups and only feel really at home with at least one other of their own kind. Hamsters are the exception—most types of hamsters are loners and should be kept alone in the pen; otherwise,

Petting can promote well-being.

Hanging out at the feeding area: fresh food is healthy and tastes delicious!

abrupt change in the animal's diet can lead to digestive problems and diarrhea.

Each small-mammal species has specific behavioral patterns. To guarantee harmonious living with your animal, you should learn what your pet is trying to tell you based on his behavior. This is also extremely important for clicker training so that you can react correctly to your animal's behavior and adjust the pace of your training if necessary.

Despite good care and grooming, your small pet can get sick, and it can be difficult to tell if your furry friend is feeling under the weather. Due to a small mammal's rapid metabolism, a seemingly mild illness can quickly become a serious emergency, such as a cold developing into lethal pneumonia. In addition, these animals try to hide signs of illness—a defense mechanism meant to protect them from predators in nature. So, by the time you notice that one of your animals is not doing well, his illness may already be in an advanced stage. If you suspect that something is wrong with one of your pets—e.g., he is behaving differently than normal or isn't eating properly—please see a veterinarian who is an expert in small mammals.

you're likely to have a battle on your hands. If you decide to get your pet a companion, it goes without saying that the animal should be from the same species. After all, you wouldn't want to spend the rest of your life with a monkey and have no contact with other humans!

Hay, vegetables, fruit, grains…find out what your pet should be eating. You will be amazed by the selection! A balanced and varied diet keeps your small pet healthy and fit. However, you should not change the basic diet too often; rather, you should supplement it with various vegetables and other healthy treats. An

Q&A

It is important not to distract your pet during training, so giving them an encouraging scratch can motivate them while staying on task.

What do I do if my pet displays positive behavior, but I don't have a clicker on hand?

>>

You can't be expected to walk around with a clicker in your pocket all day, but you can still reward your pet if he spontaneously performs a desired behavior. For example, you can praise him verbally to demonstrate your attention and approval, or you can store some emergency treats around the house where you can access them quickly if necessary (this only works, of course, with food that does not go bad!). It's OK if the click is missing between the good behavior and the reward.

Is it true that I should not talk to my animal during clicker training?

>>

Although clicker training is a playful form of training, the animal has to concentrate and think about what you are asking him to do. If you keep talking to your training partner while he's thinking, it will distract him more than help him. Of course, this does not mean you should remain silent during training; that would also be counterproductive, because being too quiet around your pet would make him feel insecure.

Finding a healthy medium is not always easy, but it is certainly the best way. Motivating the animal by using his name in a friendly way from time to time can be helpful during training, e.g., to coax him forward if he is afraid of a new obstacle. Communication with your training partner also plays an important role in teaching basic cues. Of course, you should give your small pet a lot of praise when he completes an exercise or an individual step of an exercise correctly.

If you don't have a clicker on hand, you can still reward your pet with a treat or words of encouragement.

CHAPTER 2

The Clicker Lifestyle

>>

Clicker training can be
used for all types of
animals. It is a team
activity, so it is best to
connect with your pet and
understand their learning
habits before you begin.

Clickers for All Animals

Generally, all animals can be trained using a clicker. The basic principle of conditioning to the clicker is always the same. Clickers have been used successfully for a long time to train animals actors for movies and TV—not just dogs, cats, and horses but cows, donkeys, chickens,

Tip

Proceed with Care

Rabbits and rodents are flight animals and scare very easily. Unknown sounds, like clicking, as well as hectic movements, can initially scare them. Therefore, avoid anything that could scare your pet and use a clicker with volume control if necessary.

If your small pet continues to be scared of the clicker, please do not be upset. Clicker training is a team activity, and if one of the partners doesn't feel comfortable with it, you should look for another way to spend time with your furry friend. Luckily, it's rare to find an animal who is unwilling to train, and usually nothing stands in the way of playful instruction with a pet.

Rats are sharp rodents. They learn quickly and love learning, so they are ideal pets for clicker training.

ravens, owls, and many other animals. Equally, rabbits, guinea pigs, chinchillas, rats, and other small mammals can also have fun with clickers. However, because of their size—that is, their *small* size—and the risk of running away, training is a little more difficult with hamsters and mice than it is with larger rodents and rabbits.

Despite a trainer's best efforts, there are some animals who just do not like clicker training. One of my rabbits, for example, never understood why I wanted him to jump over a hurdle when there were so many other exciting things to explore in the room.

The following are important points that you should consider during clicker training depending on the type of pet you have.

Rabbits

> Rabbits are very sensitive to stress and can be frightened easily.
> Due to their anatomy (especially their strong hind legs), rabbits are great jumpers and are therefore particularly good at clearing hurdles and doing similar types of exercises.
> Rabbits are not good climbers. Do not include exercises such as climbing a ladder, a rope, or another object in your rabbit's training plan.

Guinea Pigs

> Guinea pigs are very well suited to clicker training due to their calm nature.
> They are even-tempered and tolerant, but it is very important that you watch for the smallest signs of stress, so as not to overwhelm your guinea pig during clicker training.
> Guinea pigs have rather chubby bodies with short legs. Contrary to what you might think at first glance, they can run very quickly! However, they are not good climbers. They are also quite clumsy when jumping and can

The hurdles must be adapted to the size and condition of the respective animal. Guinea pigs are clumsy jumpers, so this hurdle is too high!

injure themselves easily, which is why you should avoid climbing exercises and only attempt low jumps with a guinea pig.

DID YOU KNOW?

Rabbits Are Not Rodents

Contrary to popular belief, rabbits do not belong to the rodent family. Their behavior and postures are quite similar to those of rodents, but they are part of the hare family (Leporidae).

Tubes made of natural materials are popular playgrounds for degus.

Degus and Chinchillas

> Both degus and chinchillas are very nimble animals who are almost always on the move. Keep this in mind when choosing your training location because your training session can easily end up as a search mission if the small rodent runs away and hides behind a cabinet. The bathroom is often a good place to train because there are fewer hiding places, but it's important to close the toilet lid so that no animals fall in!

> Degus and chinchillas love dark caves and tunnels, which is why exercises with these objects are often not difficult for them.

> Both degus and chinchillas can climb very well. With small ladders made of wood, branches, or natural ropes, you can design a diverse training course for these rodents.

Rats

> Rats have become increasingly popular as pets over the years. Their negative image as dirty disease carriers, for which the media is primarily responsible, has gradually changed as people gain better knowledge of these cute, smart animals as pets.

Tip

Recipe for Success

Before each exercise, think about whether your little friend will be able to do what you ask of him due to his species-specific characteristics. You will achieve the greatest success in clicker training with your small pets if you create training plans based on the animals' natural behaviors and abilities.

- Anyone who has spent time with rats will know that they are very social and, above all, very clever animals.
- Surely you have heard of rats quickly finding their way out of complicated labyrinths or, more recently, being used to find landmines. It is therefore not unusual that rats are particularly skilled at clicker training and learn new exercises with great enthusiasm.
- There are really no restrictions when training rats. These small rodents are skilled climbers and can also master all types of obstacles; therefore, you do not have to exclude any exercises from a rat's training plan.

Other Small Mammals
- Of course, many other rodents, like gerbils, hamsters, and mice, can be clicker trained. However, these nimble rodents can easily run away and hide under furniture or in other small spaces, so take this into account when choosing a training location. An open-air pen with a close-mesh fence is the best option.
- In principle, clicker training can be used to a certain degree with any animal—there are even reports that fish have learned to swim through tires on command with the help of clicker training. Therefore, don't be shy. Try it out and see how your animal reacts to clicker training.

They're Never Too Old

It is a widespread false belief that only young animals can learn new behaviors.

Training Times | Tip

It is best to train animals when they are already active. Under no circumstances should you wake them up for training, as this stresses them out, which makes training less effective. Some rodents, such as chinchillas and most hamsters, are mainly active in the evenings or at night, so adjust your training times accordingly.

This falsehood became clear when I was training my guinea pigs. The one who learned the fastest was Romeo, who was already five and a half years old—a relatively old age for a small mammal—when we started.

The Best Age for Training

There are not many age restrictions for training. Young animals can start training as soon as they are no longer nursing

Hamsters are nimble and can scurry away and hide during training–be sure to train them in a pen to keep them in one place.

You can start clicker training with young rabbits, but they may be easily distracted.

and are eating on their own. At this age, however, small mammals are still very easily distracted. It is terribly exciting for them to be taken out of their pens, and they often cannot really concentrate on lessons.

It has therefore proven to be helpful to wait until your pets start growing out of their "teenage" phase—that is, when they are almost fully grown—and have therefore become a little calmer. For example, the ideal age for guinea pigs and rabbits to start training is about four to six months old, and about two to four months old for rats.

With older animals, you should simply be aware that their movements can be somewhat limited. Tricks such as standing up on their hind legs (see page 63) are therefore more difficult for them than for younger animals, so do not work on these exercises if there is a risk that your pets could be injured.

Who Can Clicker Train?

We already know that clicker training is a simple method to teach your pet behaviors and behavior patterns in a playful way. As such, there are no special requirements for the trainer, provided the person understands the basic principles described in this book and can implement them with consistency, patience, and, above all, a lot of fun. It is best if the the animal is somewhat familiar with the trainer. If you have recently adopted a small pet, everyone in the home will be unfamiliar to him at first, which is why you should be particularly careful if you start training soon after bringing him home.

Children can be ideal training partners for small animals. Some of them have greater empathy for small pets than many adults do. However, even though clicker training is a fairly simple training method, and therefore well suited to children, not all children react with equal understanding and patience if their training partners do not immediately do what they are supposed to do. To avoid misunderstandings and stress for both human and animal, the first training

Familiar Faces

Tip

So that the animal does not get confused, training should initially be done only by one person; do not switch trainers frequently.

sessions with a child should be guided and supervised by an adult to make sure that the child is teaching the animal properly and not causing his or her little friend confusion or harm.

Two people can train at the same time if one focuses only on clicking and rewarding while the other uses the target stick (see chapter 4). This can make lessons easier, especially at the beginning, because each person will have fewer details to think about.

Individual or Group Training?

There is no clear answer to this question. Each animal behaves a little differently than others do, and some small mammals feel more comfortable when their cagemates take part in training sessions with them. However, animals in a group are often too distracted by their peers and therefore don't concentrate as well when training together. In addition, animals who are higher up in the group hierarchy will move to the front to get more treats while the lower-ranking animals shy away.

However, there is a clear advantage of training several animals at the same time: the imitation effect. Once one of your small training partners understands the principle of an exercise, and the others observe how he performs the desired behavior and then is rewarded for it, some of them will try to imitate the behavior to get a treat as well.

Despite this fact, I personally prefer individual training to group training. Each clicker-training session gives me the opportunity to spend time with one of

Some small mammals, such as these two friends, feel more comfortable when their cagemates take part in training sessions with them.

my furry housemates individually. During the training session, I try to address the weaknesses and strengths of my training partner as much as possible, an aspect that is often slightly neglected during group training.

During training, can there be other small pets in the room who are also conditioned to the clicker but do not take part in the lesson? If possible, there should be no other "clicker animals" in the room during training if they are not participating. It would be difficult for your other animals to understand why you are clicking but not rewarding them. If the animals hear the clicking sound too often without getting a reward, it could weaken their conditioning to the clicker.

The Training Location

Although it is possible to teach your small mammal the very first steps of clicker training while he is in his cage, this is not an ideal training location. Animals are used to being left to their own devices in their cages, so they may find it difficult to suddenly have "rules" imposed upon them in this space—not to mention that a cozy napping spot or a full food bowl can sometimes be a lot more tempting than even the most fun training session.

It is best to train with your animal in a place that he is familiar with. If you're working on an obstacle course, place the obstacles near a wall to help prevent him from running away and to help him feel more secure than he would in the middle of an open space.

It is also helpful if you always train in the same place with your little friend. After a while, your pet will associate the training location with clicker training. He will know what to expect as soon as you bring him to the training spot.

It is, of course, possible to change the training location if necessary. Don't be disappointed, however, if your pet doesn't initially perform previously learned exercises as well as he did in the old location. Location is part of the memory link between the behavior and the click/reward, so changing the location changes a key training component, which at first makes the exercise seem unfamiliar and more difficult to the animal. After a while, however—as soon as the animal recognizes the new area as a training location and is comfortable there—his confusion will disappear.

An animal with a full stomach won't be motivated to learn, so a snack right before the lesson will reduce his interest in training treats.

Rewards

Clicker training has many advantages, both for you and for your small pet (see page 12), but how do you explain to your pet that his commitment to the training sessions will be worthwhile? Simple! You have to find something that will make training feel like an achievement for the animal, starting from the very first lesson. This is where rewards come into play.

The most common, simplest, and often the most appreciated reward is food; most rodents love to eat and are happy to receive special treats. (**Note:** Avoid treats that contain sugar and molasses. Even if your animal likes them, they are harmful to his health!) Your pet will be more motivated to train if he has not just eaten a meal—if he is hungry, he will work harder to get the rewards.

That said, you must *never* let your pets go hungry just so he will work harder at

Environment Check · Tip

If you are going to train in a location unfamiliar to your pet, let the animal explore the area first. This will prevent him from getting distracted during training due to curiosity or becoming intimidated by the unknown environment.

training! Guinea pigs, rabbits, chinchillas, and the like are constant eaters. Their intestines do not have much musculature, and chewed and swallowed food is not primarily transported by intestinal contractions, as in humans, but pushed along by subsequent food. If these small animals are deprived of their food, even if only for a few hours, their entire digestive process can be disturbed, which can pose a serious danger to them. Also, if a small pet eats too much food at one time after a long gap between meals, his stomach can

Not every rodent likes to be cuddled as much our model Ida—petting as a reward is therefore not always suitable for clicker training.

Quick-Check ✔

Popular Treats for Rodents	
Dandelion	
Lettuce	
Mashed carrots (homemade or jarred baby food)	
Plain yogurt	
Pea flakes	
Sunflower seeds	
Nuts cut into quarters (nuts are very fatty, so feed sparingly)	

After a particularly successful training step, someone hit the lettuce jackpot!

become too full, possibly leading to tears in the stomach wall.

Back to the topic of treats. What trainers call a "jackpot" is a special treat that the animal receives when he does something particularly great, such as when he tries a new exercise and it goes really well. The jackpot should be something different than the regular training treats or a little larger than the usual treats, e.g., a half or a whole nut instead of a quarter of a nut.

The jackpot is meant to increase the animal's concentration for the task. He should be motivated by suddenly receiving a bigger treat than usual and, in turn, try harder in the hopes that he will hit the jackpot again. This makes training more interesting because your pet never knows when he will hit a new jackpot. In addition, the animal won't become frustrated too quickly because he knows that a treat is waiting for him if he keeps trying.

Q&A

How do I find the right rewards?

There are certainly a variety of foods that your little friend will enjoy. With clicker training, however, it is important to find your pet's absolute favorite treat so that he really gives 100 percent to get it. To find out what your pet likes best, prepare a small plate with various types of food and then offer it to him. The food that he eats first is most likely his favorite.

Here's a tip: Once you find the right reward, remove it from your pet's regular meals, if possible. For example, it is very difficult to motivate my guinea pigs with lettuce (their clicker-training reward) if they have been eating salad all day long. Instead, I give them a serving of lettuce in the morning and then other food throughout the day, so that they have a big appetite for lettuce again during evening training sessions. Whatever treats you choose, be sure to maintain a balanced diet to keep your animals healthy. Do not remove staple foods from their regular feed to use only as treats.

It is important that the reward is small enough for your pet to eat in one bite.

What's the right way to reward?

Give a reward right after every click. It is important that the reward occurs immediately after the sound so that your pet connects the reward with the click.

It is also important that the reward is small enough for your pet to eat in one bite: first, the animal will not get full too quickly; second, if a treat is too big, the animal will forget why he got the treat in the first place by the time he is finished eating it.

Your pet will be more receptive to treats if they have not just eaten a large meal—but make sure to never let them go hungry!

Another tip: Your pet may become too distracted during training if he can see the reward. In this case, you can hide the treat in your hand behind your back or, if you're using the clicker, target stick, and reward at the same time, you can place your treat container on a chair or stool.

What if my pet is shy?

>>

In theory, rewarding sounds simple, but in practice it isn't always that easy, especially if you have a very shy animal who you want to teach to be braver with the help of clicker training. Your small animal may not want to eat treats out of your hand at the beginning of training, so how can you condition an animal to the clicker when you can't reward him?

The use of the clicker has become increasingly popular in professional bird training for live shows and television.

These bird trainers have discovered the "bowl method." It works like this: The trainer clicks, places the reward in a small bowl, moves away, and waits for the bird to take the reward out of the bowl and eat it. Then the trainer repeats the process several times, gradually moving away a little less each time, making the animal more comfortable with being close to humans. A slightly modified version involves clicking when the bird has scuttled over to the bowl and is about to take the treat. However, it is important in both variations that the click sound comes before the bird pecks at the reward.

The bowl method is especially effective for birds because these feathered pets watch their humans closely and pay careful attention to every movement they make. The core of this method is the visual understanding of the treat-in-a-bowl sequence. The difficulty with small mammals, then, is that they do not see as well as birds do. If you were to place a small bowl in front of your pet and put a sunflower seed in it, the animal would most likely not even notice. However, if you place the bowl closer to the animal, he may feel pressured and not eat.

As far as I know, there is no one-size-fits-all solution for getting a shy small mammal to eat out of your hand. Up until recently, I had only one guinea pig. He was particularly anxious and initially didn't want to take any treats out of my hand. I still offered him treats from my hand every day, and, lo and behold, one day the shy guinea pig decided that he was used to the presence of my hand and came over hesitantly to get his reward.

As you can see, the key to success in this case is patience. However, you can make your pet's job easier by offering him a particularly large treat at first. This not only increases the animal's motivation, but he won't be afraid that he has to touch your hand to get the treat. To avoid contact, there is also the option of not feeding the treat directly from your hand, similar to the aforementioned method with shy birds. Instead, place the treat on a spoon or put it on a wooden skewer (without a sharp point) and carefully hold it out to your pet. You can gradually reduce the distance between your hand and the animal by using a shorter spoon or skewer or by moving your hand closer to the treat.

Find more tips on how to help your small animal build trust in you in Overcoming the Fear of Being Touched (see page 61).

The winning combination of the target stick, the clicker, and a treat results in your pet doing fun tricks and bonding with you more than ever.

CHAPTER 3

Clicker Fun

>>
Once your pet is
conditioned to the
clicker and can link it
with treats and rewards,
the joy of learning new
tricks can begin!

The Principles of Conditioning

We've already discussed the importance of conditioning to the clicker. You know that before you can use the clicker to teach your pet, he must first be conditioned to the clicker so he learns that the click is always followed by a great reward.

What Does Conditioning Mean?

> Conditioning means teaching your pet that one stimulus will be followed by another.

After just a few hours of practice, your student will understand the link: click = reward.

> Conditioning also means teaching your pet that an action is followed by a consequence.

Conditioning is a natural process, not a scientific theory created in a laboratory. In nature, conditioning to certain environmental influences plays an important role in and, in some cases, even ensures the animal's survival. Conditioning can change innate or previously learned behaviors so that a creature can better adapt to its environmental conditions.

Example: A bee looking for nectar finds more of the sweet liquid in a flower of one color than in flowers of other colors. If this happens multiple times, the bee will soon start flying only to the more bountiful flowers. In this case, there is a link between the flower color (stimulus) and the nectar (rewarding resulting from the stimulus). The bee's instinctive behavior of searching for nectar was enhanced by learning due to unconscious conditioning.

People are also conditioned to different things, and this is also completely natural and usually happens unconsciously. For example, seeing a speed trap on the highway causes many people to hit their brakes.

In clicker training, the pet is conditioned to expect a reward after the sound of the clicker. If the animal gets a reward every time he hears the click, he will soon link the sound with the positive action from you that follows it: giving him a reward.

How to Condition Your Pet

So, you bought a clicker and found your pet's "super treat" (see page 32). Now you can start the step-by-step process of conditioning your pet to the clicker.

1 Hold the clicker in your hand and let your small pet sniff the unfamiliar object to help him get used to it.

2 Press the clicker and give your pet a treat right after the click. It is important that you give the reward immediately after the click so that the animal can begin to associate the reward with the sound of the click. He needs to learn that click = reward.
   Proper timing is essential. If you give the treat at the same time as the clicking sound, the link between clicker and reward will not occur because the animal will focus only on the treat and ignore the clicking sound. However, if you wait too long after the click to give the reward, the

What's this? Allow your pet to sniff unknown objects.

animal will not be able to establish a link between the two.

3 Repeat step 2 about ten times and end your first training session by clicking and giving your pet a jackpot. This way, he will remember the training session with you and look forward to the next one.

4 Repeat the clicker conditioning exercise once or twice a day for the next few days. It's important to reiterate here that conditioning to the clicker is the basis of clicker training. If your animal does not understand that something positive happens after the click, further

training becomes very difficult. Therefore, even if you would like to progress to "real" tricks right away, be patient and reinforce the conditioning.

5 After a few days of practice, if you feel that your pet understands the exercise well, do the following: click, but wait a short moment before giving the reward. Observe your pet's behavior: is he looking around, sniffing, or reaching? Congratulations! You can proceed to the next step. Your animal understands that a reward comes after the click, and he is already waiting for his treat.

If your small animal enjoys being petted, petting him after training can help strengthen your relationship.

The Twelve Golden Rules

1 Clicker training should bring joy to people and animals. Never train your pet when you are angry or upset. Your stress will be felt by your pet, and it will intimidate him.

2 Never train with an animal who is sick or shows signs of stress.

3 Always be nice to your pet during training. Don't scold him if he does something wrong. Instead, ignore him—because scolding is a form of attention, and most animals love attention, scolding actually can be a reward for them. Scolding inadvertently reinforces unwanted behavior.

4 Every animal is different. Some learn quickly, while others learn slowly, and, in certain cases, a small mammal may never become a "clicker animal." Therefore, do not be disappointed if you encounter problems at times during training. Be patient—going too fast is a common beginner mistake.

5 If you or your pet is frustrated because an exercise isn't going well, don't despair. Take a step back in the training sequence or switch to an exercise that your pet has already learned. Try the new exercise again another day, and you should get better results. Remember that your animal will not perform at his peak every time you train.

6 Be consistent. Always do the same steps in the same order to teach and practice an exercise, or else you will confuse your little training partner.

7 Try to train with your pet in a quiet environment. Your training time should not include spectators. Only demonstrate a trick to others once your pet has mastered the behavior.

8 Work on only one exercise at a time. Wait until your animal has mastered an exercise before starting a new one.

9 Reward your pet immediately whenever he performs the behavior you want. It would be very confusing for him if you suddenly ignored him during a training session because you got distracted, for example.

10 Your pet needs to concentrate during training. Therefore, you shouldn't talk to your little training partner too much and distract him. However, if your animal is afraid of a new exercise, such as running through a tunnel, you can call him by name to encourage him.

11 A training session shouldn't be too long. You don't want your pet to become bored and lose interest. Train twice a day for fifteen minutes at a time rather than once a day for half an hour.

12 Always start each lesson by warming up with an exercise that your pet has already mastered. This way, you can reward him right from the start and set the tone for a pleasant training session. If your pet has not yet learned any exercises, start briefly with clicker conditioning before continuing with the training. You should also always end each lesson with a positive experience, so repeat an exercise or a step of an exercise that you are sure the animal has already mastered. Your pet will remember ending on a high note and will look forward to the next training session.

Additional Considerations

The exercises described in this book have been selected according to various criteria, such as level of difficulty and fun factor. Of course, there are many more exercises that you and your animal can learn. The following points will help you apply the basic clicker principles you have learned to the exercises in this book and to any new exercises that you want to try.

1 Always keep your goal in mind. Before you start the exercise, decide on the desired end result and how you plan to get there.

2 Be realistic. A guinea pig will never learn to walk on his hind legs any more than a rabbit will be able to climb

a ladder. The exercise must always suit the natural abilities and behavior of the animal.

3 Stay consistent. Once you start training a new exercise in a certain way, do not change what you are doing, as this will only confuse your pet. Changing your approach is only necessary if you are not successful after several weeks.

4 Finally, the most important rule: divide each exercise into many small steps. Otherwise, your small pet will not understand what you want from him, and you will not succeed in teaching the behavior.

Your animal will learn new exercises quickly with a target stick and clicker.

Q&A

What do I do if my pet is afraid of the clicking sound?

>>

Not all animals react calmly to the sound of the clicker when introduced to it. For example, rabbits usually react much more fearfully than guinea pigs and sometimes run from the clicker at first. Don't worry—these animals will soon learn that the clicker is completely harmless.

Follow the steps for conditioning (see pages 38–40) and allow a lot of time to accustom your pet to the sound. To soften the clicker's noise, put the clicker in your pocket. Adjustable-volume clickers are also available for animals who are particularly sensitive to noise.

If you click and reward as described in the steps, you will soon see that your pet is no longer frightened by the noise, and you can move forward with your training plan.

Take the time to condition your pet to the sound of the clicker to teach them to not be afraid of the noise.

Will my animal still remember the exercises after a four-week break, or do I have to start all over?

>>

After a long break, your animal will certainly be a little out of practice with his clicker training. However, don't assume that he has forgotten everything and that you will have to start over. You'll only need to take a few days to reacquaint your animal with the exercises.

Begin with a simple exercise, ideally one that uses a target stick (see chapter 4). Your furry friend will be a little confused at first and may not react immediately to the target stick. However, his memory will gradually return and, although you will have to go through each previously learned exercise again step by step, the learning process will be much faster than the first time.

After a long break from training, reacquaint your pet using the target stick to refresh their memory.

CHAPTER 4

Using the Target Stick

>>

The target stick is very
useful in clicker training—it
allows you to quickly repeat
and link desired behaviors
by clicking and rewarding.

Target-Stick Basics

Next to the clicker, the target stick is the most important tool in clicker training. A target stick is a handheld stick with a ball at the end, and it acts as a pointer during training. You will teach your animal to follow the target stick to get the click and subsequent reward. With the target stick, you can show your pet where you want him to run and lead him through tunnels or over bridges, for example.

Some of the following exercises can also be done without a target stick by clicking and rewarding the animal if he spontaneously performs the desired action. However, it would take a very long time for a guinea pig to figure out how to run across a seesaw on his own if you haven't first shown him with the target stick. And, even if your pet does spontaneously perform the behavior (e.g., walking across the seesaw), and

you click and reward him, it is unlikely that he will understand the connection between his action and the reward. The target stick allows you to quickly repeat and link desired behaviors by showing approval (clicking and rewarding). The target stick is very useful in clicker training.

You may not find target sticks in your local pet-supply store, but they are easy to find online. It is also very easy to make a target stick yourself.

I used a chopstick to make my target stick, but you can use a stick made of any nontoxic material, such as a branch or a thick skewer without a sharp tip. Place a small ball on one end of the stick; a soft foam rubber ball is best because you can easily poke a hole in it. This type of ball is available in craft and toy stores or even in pet-supply stores as cat toys.

Target sticks are easy to make with nontoxic materials such as chopsticks, branches, or even a skewer.

If you want, you can paint your target stick. However, use only nontoxic paint in case your little friend nibbles on the stick.

Stage 1: Touching the Target Stick

1 Hold the target stick with the ball tip close to your pet's nose. The ball must not touch the animal.

2 Watch your little friend's reaction. If he looks curiously at the target stick, click and immediately give him his reward.

3 Briefly remove the target stick after each click before showing it to the animal again. The first time he touches the ball, reward him with a jackpot; click and reward all subsequent touches.

4 Repeat steps 1–3 a few times. When your pet is confidently touching the ball, try holding the target stick a little to the right or left. Click and reward when he touches the ball.

5 When your pet is consistent with step 4, hold the target stick a little over his head so that he must lift his head to touch the ball. When he does, click and reward.

Your pet may find it difficult at first when you hold the target stick over his head because it is no longer at his level or because he is having trouble seeing it. If this is the case with your pet, and he refuses to lift his head to touch the target stick, you can skip this part of the

Your pet should touch the ball at the tip of the target stick with his nose or mouth.

exercise and go straight to stage 2 (on page 48). When your pet has learned to follow and reach for the target stick, he will also stretch up to touch the ball.

Air Them Out

Tip

If using foam rubber balls to make target sticks, take them out of their packaging and let them air out for a few days before you work with them. Some animals may shy away from the smell of the foam.

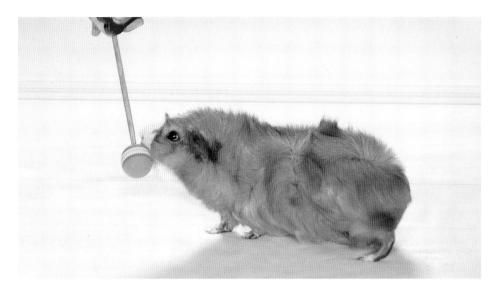

You did it! The first steps of target-stick training are a success.

Stage 2: Reaching for the Target Stick

1 Hold the target stick farther away but still close enough that your pet can touch it without walking toward the target stick.

2 If your little training partner stretches for the target stick and nudges the ball, click and reward.

3 Repeat this exercise until it is consistent. Then move on to stage 3.

Stage 3: Walking toward the Target Stick

1 Hold the target stick in front of your small pet so that he must stretch to touch the ball. Click and reward your animal when he touches the target stick.

2 Next, hold the target stick the same way as in step 1 but far enough away that your pet must take a step forward to be able to touch it. If your training partner hesitates at first, give him some encouragement in a soft voice.

Tip

The Right Perspective

Eyes on either side of their heads allow rodents and rabbits to see well in all directions, but they can't see very far into the distance. In addition, rabbits do not see in full color and can only distinguish red and green.

If your animal doesn't follow the target stick, he may just not have seen it properly. Tap the ground lightly with the target stick to get your pet's attention. This trick worked well with my guinea pig Oliver.

Following the target stick up an incline is a popular expansion on targeting.

3 Reward your pet with a jackpot the first time he walks to touch the target stick.

4 Gradually increase the distance between the target stick and the animal. At first, he needs to take only a step or two to touch the stick and get the reward, but later he must cover more distance.

Some small animals initially have problems following the target stick around. To make the exercise easier for your pet, start by guiding him in only one direction, e.g., along the length of the wall. If your pet runs this route confidently, you can add one curve, then several curves, and then progress to guiding him around the entire training area.

Introduction to Obstacle Courses

Once your animal has learned to follow the target stick well, start guiding him over various obstacles, like bridges and seesaws. You can use the different obstacles to build a small playground for your pet. Remember to always match the training course to your animal's natural physical abilities so that your pet does not get hurt.

In chapter 5, some of the obstacle-course exercises, including the seesaw and the tunnel, are explained in more detail. The procedure for setting up these obstacles can be applied to everything you want to include in your small pet's playground.

Q&A

What if my pet won't touch the target stick?

Every animal is unique. Learning ability and speed of learning not only differ from species to species and breed to breed but also from animal to animal. Some small animals learn to follow the target stick after the first lesson, while others need several weeks.

But what do I do to encourage my pet to touch the target stick?

First of all, remember one of the most important rules of clicker training: be patient! If you are tense or impatient during training, you will impede your pet's progress.

Now, hold the target stick close to your training partner as usual. However, this time, don't wait for him to touch it; instead, click when he turns his head toward the target stick or makes another movement to indicate that he has seen the target stick and is paying attention.

If your pet touches the target stick but does not specifically hit the ball at the tip, you can reward this action at first. After a few training sessions, however, you should stop doing this and only reward him for touching the ball. Your animal will soon understand that, from now on, he must touch the ball at the end of the target stick to get his reward.

You will see, little by little, that your pet will become more and more interested in the ball on the target stick. Once he is consistently touching it, you can move forward with your training plan.

If your pet is having trouble with the target stick, click and reward when they touch any part of the stick, and then only when they touch the tip. Soon they will link the ball with the reward.

Although you can technically use your hand instead of a target stick, this will likely cause confusion later down the line.

Can my pet follow my hand instead of the target stick?

Ultimately, it doesn't matter whether you use a target stick or simply use your hand for targeting when performing an exercise. The animal will learn to follow and touch your hand just as he would with the target stick.

However, does it really make sense to teach your pet to focus on your hand like this? Imagine that you reach into the cage, and your animal runs toward you and nudges your hand. You just wanted to put some food in the bowl! And what will your animal think if he demonstrates a learned behavior but does not receive a reward? For this reason, I personally think it is better to use a target stick during training so that misunderstandings do not occur.

Does every animal need his own target stick?

When an animal touches the tip of the target stick or even bites into it during training, he involuntarily transfers his scent to the target stick. For animals who live together in the same cage or room, and are therefore used to each other's perfume, this will not be a problem. If the small animals are not familiar with each other, it is better to use a separate target stick for each animal. This way, your four-legged friend will not be distracted by a strange smell on the target stick and can concentrate better on clicker training.

Animal scents are transferred onto the target stick—so make sure not to share the stick with animals who are not familiar with each other. The smell can be a distraction!

CHAPTER 5

The Target Stick: Your Magic Wand

>>

Once your pet is
fully conditioned and
comfortable with the
training stick, you can use
it to lead them through
hurdles, mazes, and
jumps with ease.

Exercises with a Target Stick

Before you start the various target-stick exercises, be sure that your animal has mastered the basics of clicker training. He should be adequately conditioned to the clicker and be able to follow the target stick and touch the ball on the end. Without these basics, you cannot teach your animal the following behaviors and tricks.

When in doubt, continue the basic target training for another day or two. It is always better to go slower than too fast. An animal who is overwhelmed and does not understand what is required of him quickly becomes frustrated and unwilling to learn.

SLALOM

Suitable for: All small pets
Difficulty level: Easy
Tools needed: Target stick, clicker, treats, obstacles to make a slalom course

Do not use any obstacles that could cause injury (such as items with sharp edges) if an animal bumps into them. Suitable objects include empty toilet paper rolls, empty plastic cups, or blocks. The size of the objects should be appropriate to the size of the animal. For example, a rabbit won't understand why he should

One Step at a Time   Tip

The following exercises are divided into steps, which you should perform in the given sequence with your pet. However, please note that you should only move on to the next step once your pet fully understands the step you are working on. Sometimes this can take a day, but sometimes it can take a week or more.

run around a building block when he could simply jump over it and get to his destination much faster.

This exercise is similar to target-stick training (beginning on page 46). Therefore, it is a good introductory exercise, and you should make progress quickly.

How it's done:

1 Place three to four slalom obstacles in a straight line. Based on the animal's size, allow enough distance between the objects so that the animal will not touch them when weaving through them.

2 Guide your pet around the first obstacle in the tightest possible curve with the help of the target stick. Click and reward him when he touches the ball at the tip of the target stick.

3 Next, your pet should not touch the target stick immediately after the first obstacle. Hold the target stick in front of your animal and guide him until he is almost all the way around the second obstacle. Once he has circled the second obstacle, hold the target stick still so that he can touch it, then click and reward as usual. Unlike in target-stick training, where you held the target stick in one spot, you are now moving the target stick away from the animal until he reaches the goal.

4 Repeat step 3, each time guiding your little friend around one more obstacle before he touches the target stick to receive his click and reward. It is important that you increase the length of his path step by step, taking plenty of time. Asking your pet to cover too much distance at the beginning or trying to lead him over the entire slalom course from the start can cause the animal to get frustrated and confused because he will not understand why he is not allowed to touch the target stick.

5 When your little training partner gets through the entire slalom course, reward him with a jackpot after the click. You can then gradually add more obstacles to the slalom.

Step by step through the slalom: no problem for Oliver the guinea pig!

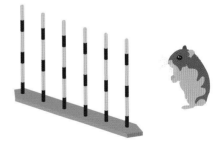

RUNNING THROUGH A TUNNEL

Suitable for: All small pets
Difficulty level: Easy
Tools needed: Tunnel, target stick, clicker, treats

The diameter of the tunnel must be suitable for the size of the animal. The tunnel preferably should be made of wood, but other materials, such as plastic or cardboard, are also acceptable. Flexible bridges, made of willow sticks connected with wire and available in various sizes from pet-supply stores, are particularly suitable for small pets. Because they are bendable, you can use them to form arches, tunnels, and tubes.

Running through a tunnel is a simple enough trick; building your pet's confidence will make them less anxious during some of the harder exercises.

Even if this exercise seems very simple at first, it takes a lot of care and sensitivity to get an anxious animal to follow the target stick through a tunnel. Although rabbits and rodents are cave dwellers, some pets are still afraid to walk through narrow, unfamiliar passages.

Small animals who like to slip through small openings or who already have tunnels or tubes in their cages will have no problems with this exercise. For these animals, this exercise makes a good introduction to training because they should be successful right away.

How it's done:

1 Place the tunnel on the ground and let your pet sniff and examine the new object on his own.

2 Once your animal is familiar with the obstacle, use the target stick to lead

Clicker Training for Rabbits, Guinea Pigs, and Other Small Pets

him as close as possible to the tunnel entrance. If he touches the ball on the target stick, click and reward.

3 Now hold the target stick inside the tunnel so that your pet has to stick his head inside to touch the ball on the end. Click and reward immediately when he does. It is best to place the target stick into the tunnel on the side opposite where your pet is standing so that your hand will not be in his way and he will not feel pressured.

4 Repeat step 3, gradually placing the target stick a little deeper into the tunnel until your pet has to take a few steps into the dark tunnel to touch the ball. When he does, click and reward with a jackpot.

5 Slowly increase the distance between the tunnel entrance and the target stick until your pet has to walk all the way through the tunnel to get to the target stick. When he touches the ball, click and reward with a jackpot.

HIDING UNDER A BLANKET

Suitable for: All small pets
Difficulty level: Easy
Tools required: Thin blanket or towel, target stick, clicker, treats

Normally, this exercise is met with no difficulty from most animals, especially if they have already learned to follow the target stick through a tunnel, because the

Teaching your pet to hide under a blanket is a cozy, easy lesson, since most animals naturally love the feeling.

basic structure of this exercise is the same as the tunnel exercise. Many animals like to hide under blankets when they're playing. Rodents and rabbits also love cozy caves.

It is important that you do not leave the room during this exercise. If your small pet is under a blanket, he could easily be overlooked by another person coming into the room. If someone accidentally steps on the blanket, it could be fatal to your animal!

How it's done:

1 Place the blanket (or towel) loosely on the floor so that there is an opening on at least one side.

2 Guide your animal to one of the openings with the target stick. If he touches the ball, click and reward.

3 Now use the target stick to guide the animal into the opening. When he touches the ball, click and reward with a jackpot.

4 Work in small increments until your training partner is all the way under the blanket. Reward his great achievement with a jackpot!

WALKING ON A SEESAW

Suitable for: All small pets (see note)
Difficulty level: Easy to medium
Tools required: Seesaw, target stick, clicker, treats

Note: This exercise is more difficult for larger and less nimble animals like guinea

Less nimble pets such as guinea pigs will find this a bit more challenging than rabbits or rats. After a little practice, the tilting movement of the seesaw will no longer be scary.

pigs because they cannot balance well and have to first overcome their fear of the moving seesaw.

You can make a seesaw by placing a board on top of a stick, for example. However, be careful that the board cannot slip. Attach the two pieces together if necessary. You can also buy a seesaw at the pet-supply store. Whatever you use for a seesaw, make sure that your animal cannot get stuck anywhere in or under it.

Initially, you should practice this exercise only in one direction, e.g., going up the right side of the seesaw and back down on the left. Only when your animal has learned this training sequence consistently should you start guiding him in the other direction. This will make your pet's learning process easier, with no misunderstandings.

How it's done:

1 Place the seesaw on the floor and let your animal get used to the new object. He might run across the seesaw right away out of sheer curiosity.

2 Once your pet has examined the new obstacle extensively, guide him with the target stick to stand in front of the seesaw so that he has to put his front feet on the board to be able to touch the ball on the target stick. When he does, click and reward.

3 Repeat step 2 a few times, holding the target stick farther away from your pet, a little at a time, so that he has to walk onto the seesaw to get his click and treat. If it goes well the first time he has all four feet on the seesaw, click and reward with a jackpot.

4 Next, slowly guide your animal over the seesaw with the help of the target stick. If you can get your pet to touch the target stick at the moment when the seesaw begins to tip, you can click and reward him right away—and the treat will ease the shock your pet will experience when the board suddenly moves under his feet.

5 You can now guide your animal gradually over the entire seesaw. The first time he is successful, reward him with a jackpot after the click.

TURNING IN CIRCLES

Suitable for: All small pets
Difficulty level: Easy
Tools required: Target stick, clicker, treats

When you begin to teach this exercise, limit yourself to one direction at first, meaning that the animal always turns to the right or always turns to the left. This will make the learning process easier for your small pet.

How it's done:

1 Place your pet on the ground in front of you and hold the target stick slightly to one side of his head. If your animal turns his head to touch the ball at the tip of the stick, click and reward.

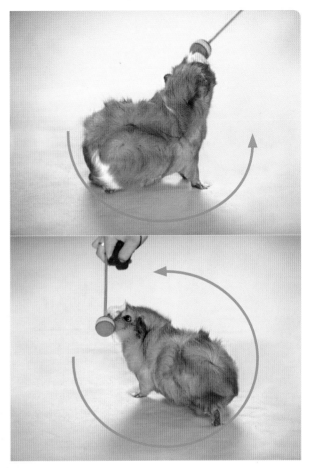

First a half circle, then a whole circle. As always, the target stick guides your smart pet.

2 Next, instead of holding the target stick just a little to the side of your pet's head, as you did in step 1, move the pointer slowly farther to the side so that he can no longer touch it by only turning his head. Move the stick so your animal has to take a few short steps, starting to turn in a circle, to touch the ball. When he does, click and reward. If this step doesn't work right away, don't worry.

Many small animals need a little time to understand why they should follow the target stick when it is at the edge of their field of vision.

3 When step 2 is going well, you can start to move the target stick all the way around the animal. If he follows the target stick to turn in a full circle and

If you have a guinea pig, practice climbing or jumping over low hurdles with him instead of jumping through a hoop.

then touches the ball at the end, click and reward.

JUMPING THROUGH A HOOP

Suitable for: Rabbits, degus, chinchillas, and other small pets who like to jump
Difficulty level: Medium
Tools required: Ring or hoop (such as a child-sized hula hoop or something similar that is easy to handle), target stick, clicker, treats

Although rabbits and some rodents are good jumpers, make sure the obstacle isn't too high; you don't want your pet to injure himself. In *Kaninhop* (rabbit show jumping), a sport in which rabbits jump over obstacles, the maximum jump height for "elite" rabbits in European competition is 20 inches (about 50cm). However, I recommend much lower jumps for your pet rabbit! With smaller animals, like chinchillas and degus, jumps must be even lower so that the animals can easily get over them. *Never*—even if you get frustrated—push your pet over the obstacle if he hesitates to jump.

How it's done:

1 Hold the hoop upright, resting on the ground, in front of your pet. Leave a distance of at least 12 inches (30cm) between the hoop and the animal to allow your pet a short running start so he does not have to jump from a standstill. This is recommended, especially at the beginning of the exercise, because your

animal might otherwise refuse to jump. A running start can help reduce your pet's fear and help him confidently jump through the hoop.

2 Guide your little performer through the hoop with the target stick. Click and reward immediately when he touches the target stick.

3 Now, hold the hoop just ½ inch (about 1cm) off the ground so that the animal can still climb through it easily. If your pet succeeds and touches the target stick, click and reward.

4 Hold the hoop a little higher each time. Eventually, the hoop will be too high for your pet to climb over, and he will have to take a small jump. When he does this for the first time, click and reward with a jackpot.

OVERCOMING THE FEAR OF BEING TOUCHED

Suitable for: Any pet who is afraid of being touched
Difficulty level: Easy to very difficult, depending on the severity of the animal's fear
Tools required: Target stick, clicker, treats

This exercise goes hand in hand with the frequently asked "How can I hand-tame my animal?" If a small mammal does not allow himself to be touched, you can assume that he is not yet tame and is still afraid of humans. It should be noted,

Feeding your pet from your lap helps diminish his fear of humans.

however, that different types of small pets develop relationships differently with their humans. For example, while rabbits usually become very affectionate after a short time, mice prefer to keep their distance. Therefore, you should find out what behavior is typical for your animal so that you know what to expect and can be prepared (Go to chapter 2 to learn about your pet's learning behaviors).

Animals become a little bit more trusting each time they have positive experiences with their humans. For this reason, the exercises explained in the previous chapter also help your animal option to stop, or else he will easily panic and will not become tame.

How it's done:

1 Sit down on the floor with your pet and let him run around you undisturbed. Avoid making jerky movements so that the animal doesn't get scared. To calm the anxious animal, speak to him in a low, soothing voice.

2 Next, bring your pet as close as possible to you with the target stick. If he touches the ball of the target stick near you, click and reward.

Note: This is often easier said than done. If your animal is very fearful of you, he will only be able to approach you slowly and nervously. For this reason, is important that you are particularly careful and patient. Guide him to you only a little at a time.

3 If the animal hesitates and doesn't yet get close to you, click and reward him anyway. You will see that if you repeat this exercise often enough, the distance between you and your animal will continue to decrease until your training partner is sitting right in front of you.

4 Next, place your hand flat on the floor and slowly guide your pet closer to it. The goal of this exercise is for the animal to put his front feet on your hand to touch the ball at the tip of the target stick. The first time he does this, click and reward with a jackpot.

become less and less afraid of you. It is very important that you are able to pick up and hold your animal without stressing him, e.g., during a routine examination, when cleaning the cage, or when caring for him if he gets sick.

In addition to clicker training, there is also the classic method of getting your animal to gain trust in you: if you spend a lot of time with him, he will eventually become tamer. This means feeding him out of your hand multiple times per day and speaking calmly to him. The technique for teaching your pet to eat out of your hand is similar to other methods in clicker training; be patient, use a calm tone, and use the time to bond with your pet.

Remember that clicker training is meant to be a choice for your animal. You should never forget this, especially during this exercise! It is important that your animal approaches you and not vice versa. Your small pet must always have the

5 Repeat step 4 by placing your hand on the floor, but not flat—for example, move the tips of your fingers to create a kind of hill. If the animal is not afraid of this, click and reward.

6 Now move your hand slowly on the floor instead of holding it still. With your hand moving slightly, repeat the process in step 4. If your pet touches the ball on the target stick, click and reward.

7 When you are successful with the previous step, you can start to integrate your body into your animal's obstacle course—you can become a living obstacle, so to speak. Use the target stick to guide your small pet along your arm or to get him to jump onto your lap. As you make progress, your animal becomes more and more comfortable around you. Reward bigger achievements with a click and a jackpot; small successes earn your pet a click and a small reward.

STANDING UP ON HIND LEGS

Suitable for: All small pets (see note)
Difficulty: Easy if teaching the animal to stand up to reach the target stick; difficult if teaching the animal to stand up on cue
Tools required: Target stick, clicker, treats

Note: Older animals are often less athletic and have difficulty standing up on their own. Also, guinea pigs have a much harder time balancing on two feet than rabbits do.

You can make the exercise easier for your pet by holding out your hand or a finger or by building a small "pedestal" for him to lean on. With this type of help, even my guinea pig Romeo learned to stand up straight despite having limited mobility after a thighbone fracture.

The cue word (sometimes called the "command") is introduced in step 5 of the exercise. The goal in cue training is to be able to complete the exercise without the target stick so that your rodent

First, teach your pet to stand on his hind legs with the target stick. Next, introduce the cue word along with the target stick, then the cue word alone.

Just Try It

See if your animal enjoys cue training and makes progress. Keep in mind that larger animals, like rabbits, guinea pigs, and especially rats, learn verbal cues more easily, but don't be disappointed if you have little or no success. Instead, be happy that you can get your pet to do tricks with the target stick.

stands up after hearing the cue word. However, keep in mind that performing on cue is a very demanding task for your little friend, one that not all animals are capable of doing. Not every dog can become a police dog, even with the proper training. In any case, you need a lot of patience: cue training for a single exercise with a small animal can take several months or even longer, although some will understand the verbal cue after just a few weeks.

How it's done:

1 First, with your animal on the floor, present him with the target stick as usual. When he touches the ball at the tip of the target stick, click and reward.

2 Now hold the target stick over the animal's head so that he must stretch a little to touch it. When he does, click and reward.

3 Slowly move the target stick higher and higher over the animal's head. Be

sure that you are holding the target stick directly over your pet's body so that he is not tempted to run forward to reach the target stick. When he touches the ball, click and reward.

4 When your pet lifts his front feet for the first time, even if only for the briefest moment, click and reward with a jackpot.

5 When your pet has learned to stand up on his hind legs to touch the target stick, choose a verbal cue that you want to use for this exercise from now on. The word should be short, to the point, and something that you don't use all the time; some examples are "lift" or "stand." You might even pick a foreign-language word that you rarely use in everyday life. Once you have chosen a word, say it clearly every time your animal stands up to touch the ball on the target stick, then click and reward.

6 After you have been practicing the exercise for a while using the cue word, you can test whether your animal reacts to it: say the cue word while your pet is sitting on the floor and see what happens. If your animal actually stands, or at least looks, up, click and give him an extra-special jackpot. If your pet does not respond to the cue, never scold him. Maybe he just needs a little more time to link the word with the action, so continue practicing step 5. Even if you no longer want to train your pet to verbal cues, you can still use the cue word when practicing this exercise with the target stick. As your

small pet becomes a hardworking clicker animal, he may also listen to your cues at some point in the future—who knows?

COMING ON CUE

Suitable for: All small pets (see note)
Difficulty level: Medium to difficult
Tools required: Target stick, clicker, treats

Note: It is helpful if the animal is already tame and comfortable with humans when you start this exercise.

It's not only dogs and cats who recognize their names. Perhaps you have heard of rodents who run to their owners when called. Or maybe you own a guinea pig who hurries to the edge of his cage as soon as he hears your footsteps or your voice. This behavior is a result of (mostly unconscious) training. The animal has learned to associate something positive with your voice, for example, if you say your pet's name each time you feed him. As a result, he has been conditioned to your voice and now expects something tasty every time he hears you, and therefore gets excited when he sees you.

As you can see, the basic principles of clicker training—and, in this case, specifically those of cue training—can also be found in a pet's everyday life and are based on his natural, innate behavior. This example also shows very clearly that a lot of patience leads to success, even with difficult cues.

Only after plenty of training can you test if your pet will come to you when called without the help of the target stick.

How it's done with a target stick:

1 Sit on the floor about 12 inches (30cm) away from your pet at the beginning of the exercise.

2 Guide your pet toward you with the target stick until he is right in front of

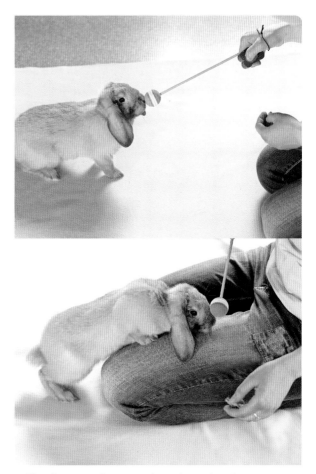

The Come on Cue exercise takes a lot of practice before your pet will respond consistently. Use the cue word along with the target stick to reinforce the behavior.

you. You can move the target stick close to your body so that he must put his paws on your leg or hand to be able to touch the end of the stick and get his click and reward. The advantage of doing this is that you can click and reward your pet for something more specific than just being somewhere on the floor.

3 Every time your pet comes to you, say your cue word clearly.

4 Once you have repeated steps 1–3 often enough that your pet is responding consistently, try to do the exercise without a target stick. Sit on the floor next to your pet, let him walk around a bit, and watch him. When he is no longer busy exploring the area, say the cue word. With a bit of luck, your pet will come curiously over to you to get his click and reward. However, your training partner may not react at all—don't be disappointed. For most rabbits and rodents, learning to come on cue is not as difficult as learning to stand up on their hind legs on cue. Nevertheless, it is still a task that, like all cue exercises, requires a lot of patience and perseverance.

How it's done without a target stick:

1 If your pet happens to be walking in your direction on his own, say the cue word clearly and click while he is coming toward you. When he gets to you, give him the treat.

2 Once you are successful with step 1, start calling your pet with the cue word when he is not already on his way to you. The first time your pet responds correctly, reward him with a jackpot. **Note:** Do not call your pet to come if he is eating or sleeping.

3 Gradually increase the distance between you and your pet.

GIVE ME FIVE

Suitable for: All small pets (see note)
Difficulty level: Medium
Tools required: Target stick, clicker, treats

Note: It's easier to teach this trick to larger animals, such as rabbits and guinea pigs.

How it's done:

1 Hold the target stick over your pet's head so that he must stretch to touch it.

2 If your pet lifts a foot because he wants to stand up, lightly touch his foot from below with your finger, click at the same moment, and then reward. **Tip:** This exercise is often easier if you've already trained the animal to stand up on his hind legs.

3 Repeat step 2 a few times. Your pet will begin to understand that he must put his foot on your finger to get his

Give Me Five is a popular exercise to show off to your friends.

treat. Then, you can start to try it without the target stick. Just offer your animal a finger and then click and reward if he puts his foot on it.

4 Gradually, you can turn your finger to point upward so that the movement looks like a real high five. In addition, you can introduce a verbal cue so that your animal puts his foot on your finger when you ask him to "give me five." The Give Me Five exercise is a fun trick even without a cue word; it's a good one to show your friends if you want to put on a little show with your pet.

Give Me Ten

Tip

Some animals, especially some rabbits, will have difficulty touching your finger with only one paw. If this is the case with your pet, convert the Give Me Five exercise into Give Me Ten—teach your pet to put both front feet on your finger instead of just one.

CHAPTER 6

Tricks with Clicks

There are some
exercises that are
best done using
only the clicker.

Exercises without a Target Stick

Although the target stick was required for the exercises in chapter 5, do not use a target stick to teach the exercises in this chapter. Instead, you will click for spontaneous behavior that is not guided by a target stick. Some of the following exercises aim to make the animal behave passively and *not* do something (e.g., not scratching when you pick him up) instead of teaching him to actively perform an action. This passive behavior is understandably difficult to express with the target stick. Nevertheless, the exercises in this chapter can be taught just as effectively and are just as easy to understand as the training exercises with the target stick.

Rabbits in particular are usually very enthusiastic about playing soccer.

PLAYING SOCCER

Suitable for: Larger rodents and rabbits
Difficulty level: Easy to medium
Tools needed: Ball, clicker, treats

The ball should not be too small, and your pet should be able to push it comfortably with his head and get it rolling. The method of teaching this exercise is very similar to target-stick training.

How it's done:

1 Place the ball on the floor in front of your pet. If he seems interested in it or sniffs at it, click and reward. Just like with target-stick training, your animal is being conditioned and rewarded with a click and treat whenever he touches the ball with his nose.

2 If he pushes the ball a little, it will start to roll. When this happens, reward the animal with a jackpot after the click.

3 From now on, click and reward only if the ball wobbles or rolls a bit after your pet touches it. He must make the ball move to get the reward.

4 Repeat steps 3 and 4 until your animal understands the connection: moving ball = click and reward.

PLAYING BASKETBALL

Suitable for: Mainly rabbits
Difficulty level: Easy to medium
Tools required: Small lattice ball (see note), clicker, treats

Note: Look for a small lattice ball for cats or birds and made of something other than plastic, as your rabbit can easily destroy a plastic ball.

This exercise is especially good for rabbits because they naturally do the required movements. When I got my first rabbit, I often saw him picking up small objects, like tissue packets and crumpled paper, with his teeth and tossing them up in the air with a jerky motion. This game was especially fun for the rabbit when he was up on the couch because the object would fall to the floor, and I would have to pick it up and give it to him to throw again. I encouraged this "basketball" game with the help of the clicker so that it eventually became something he could do independently.

The following instructions assume that your animal has not previously shown the behavior of throwing objects in the air on his own.

Important: If you hold the ball in front of the rabbit (as in step 3) and want to draw his attention to it, carefully touch the rabbit's nose with the ball. It is important that you do not touch your rabbit's neck with the ball because this is

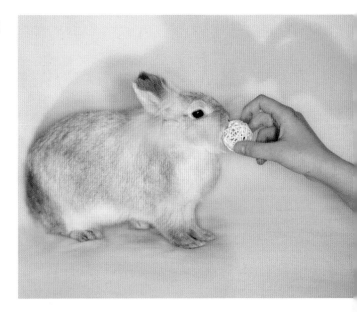

A lattice ball made of natural material is perfect for your rabbit to toss in the air.

a very sensitive area. Most rabbits flinch when touched on the neck because in nature a bite on the neck from a predator can mean death. In order to avoid such misunderstandings when training your rabbit, always hold the ball above your rabbit's nose.

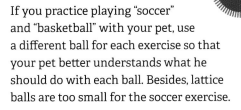

Ball Games

Tip

If you practice playing "soccer" and "basketball" with your pet, use a different ball for each exercise so that your pet better understands what he should do with each ball. Besides, lattice balls are too small for the soccer exercise.

How it's done:

1 Hold the ball (or another object that your rabbit can grasp well with his front teeth) in front of your rabbit and draw attention to the ball by waving it around slightly.

2 When the rabbit notices the ball, looks at it, or sniffs it, click and reward.

3 If your rabbit tries to bite the ball when you hold it directly in front of his nose or even just lightly touches the ball, click and reward with a jackpot.

4 You cannot teach the actual throwing movement; however, it will inevitably occur when the rabbit picks up the ball and then drops it. When he does this for the first time, click and reward with a jackpot.

HOUSE-TRAINING WITH A CLICK

Suitable for: All small pets; works particularly well with rabbits
Difficulty level: Medium
Tools required: Litter box, litter, clicker, treats

Many pet owners want to teach their small pets to be house-trained, and it is actually not that difficult. There are several approaches to showing your small animal that he should do his business only in the litter box. Use the clicker-training method presented here

only with an animal who trusts you and does not mind being lifted and carried by you.

The first step is to choose a litter box. You can use a cat litter box or a litter box designed for small animals; both are suitable and available in different styles. Some models have covers, while others consist of a tray that is accessible from all sides. The advantage of a covered litter box is that the animal can't flick as much dirty litter outside of the box. On the other hand, urine odors accumulate under the cover, which can disturb a rabbit's sensitive nose and prevent him from wanting to use the litter box again. It makes sense to purchase different types because you'll need at least two litter boxes: one for the play area and one for the cage. Buying different litter boxes will help you determine which style your pet prefers.

For your small pet, use wood shavings, straw pellets, or straw litter at the bottom of the litter box. Avoid cat litter of any kind, as eating it would be poisonous to your pet. Further, clumping litter will expand in your small animal's stomach, which could lead to death. If you clean the litter boxes regularly, the recommended types of small-animal litter can absorb most smells.

In addition to the proper supplies, you also need more patience than usual with this exercise! To avoid having to keep your animals exclusively in their pen for a long time or having to separate them, it is best to house-train your rodent or rabbit along with their roommates—and that takes time. It's best to start training when you have several days off and can devote yourself fully to your animals.

Training in a group also means that only one training partner should be conditioned to the clicker so as not to affect the other animals' learning. Can you now house-train only one of the animals in the group? No. There is a trick: condition each of the other animals to different clicks by using different clickers with different sounds. Each animal gets his own click of approval! You can now decide whether to train the animals one after the other or try to use several clickers in the same training session to give the animals individual approval when they show the desired behavior. The following training method is an example for one animal.

How it's done in the pen:

1 Place the litter box in a corner of the pen and put some of your pet's droppings in the litter box so that he immediately gets an idea of what this new area will be used for.

2 Watch your animal closely. He likely has a preferred corner where he goes

Litter box or hutch? Small misunderstandings can arise at the beginning of training.

to relieve himself—most rabbits and rodents do. If the litter box is in this corner, your pet will definitely go to the litter box to continue doing his business in his preferred spot. If your animal relieves himself in the designated potty area, click and reward when he exits the litter box.

3 If you notice that your pet is doing his business in another corner of the pen, either move the litter box to that corner or set up several litter boxes.

4 Keep watching your pet. Every time he is about to urinate or defecate in the wrong place inside the pen, put him in his litter box right away. (**Tip:** If you cannot easily pick up your pet, you can direct him toward the litter box with the target stick.) If he then successfully does his business in the litter box, click and reward immediately. Remember that house-training requires you to have lot of patience and to observe your pet

carefully. You will soon find that you know exactly when your pet is about to relieve himself. For example, most rabbits move backward and lift their tails slightly before defecating.

How it's done outside the pen:

1 Depending on the size of the area, you will have to set up several litter boxes. If your small animal feels that nature is calling, and he cannot see a litter box close by, he will use your carpet as a toilet despite his training. Just like when house-training in the pen, you'll need to be flexible when setting up litter boxes. If your pet has a preferred potty spot in the room, place the litter box there and put some of the rodent's droppings in the box.

Note: Sometimes, placing a litter box in the animal's preferred spot is not possible—for example, if he chooses to hide under the bed to relieve himself. The easiest way around this is to make such places inaccessible to the animal, such as by blocking them off with pillows. It may help to place a bowl of healthy treats in the spot to distract your pet.

2 Watch your animal run around freely. If he uses one of the litter boxes, click and reward him while he's still in the box.

3 If he does his business (or starts to do his business) in the wrong place, quickly place him in a litter box. If he relieves himself there, click and reward.

4 Keep repeating steps 2 and 3. The more often you can reward your pet for the desired behavior, the sooner he will establish a connection between the litter box and the reward. However, there are also animals who, despite all efforts, do not become house-trained.

Common Mistakes in House-Training

When you watch your rodent, you really need to give him your undivided attention. You can't watch TV, read a book, tidy up, crochet, or make phone calls and still watch your pet closely. Your training partner needs his click and reward after every successful visit to the litter box (or as many as possible) as well as gentle reminders to use the litter box if he wants to do his business in the wrong place.

Admittedly, house-training is not an incredibly exciting exercise. Nevertheless, you have to take time and always remain patient, even if the animal does not seem to grasp the concept after several hours of practice. Do not consider watching your pets as a chore, but as an opportunity to get to know them better. It allows you to better understand the social life and behavior patterns of your rodents.

GETTING USED TO BEING PICKED UP

Suitable for: All small pets (see note)
Difficulty level: Medium
Tools required: Clicker, treats, someone to act as a training assistant

Note: The requirement for this exercise is that the animal is only afraid of being picked up, not afraid of human contact in general. Otherwise, you have to start with Overcoming the Fear of Being Touched (see page 61).

Stress-free lifting is the prerequisite for relaxed handling of your animal.

Do not lift your rabbit or rodent by the neck. This can be painful for the animal and causes stress because it is similar to being grabbed by a bird of prey. The pen is a good place to train because you do not want your animal to be afraid when you pick him up from the pen.

How it's done:

1 Carefully touch your pet under the belly. If he stays calm, without scratching you or fidgeting, click and reward.

2 Hold your animal under the belly with one hand, support his hind feet with the other hand, and carefully lift him an inch or so (about 3cm) off the ground. At the same time, say a word you have chosen for this exercise, such as "up." In this exercise, the word does not serve as the actual cue; instead, it "explains" to your animal what is happening. If you say the same word every time you pick him up, your pet will soon know what happens to him when he hears the familiar word. If he behaves calmly, your assistant clicks and rewards.

3 Put the animal back on the floor and say a different word, such as "down." If your pet remains calm and his feet touch the ground, your training assistant clicks and rewards. The first time this happens, your pet gets a jackpot.

4 If your little training partner fidgets when you are trying to put him down, wait a few seconds for him to become calm. He will only get his click and reward if he doesn't fidget when you are putting him down. Of course, you should not just keep your pet hanging out in mid-air for a long time if he is afraid. If your pet just won't stop fidgeting and scratching, set him down carefully, but without clicking or rewarding. Do not say or do anything to express displeasure. Instead, walk away and ignore him for a short time. Plan to repeat the exercise later.

5 Practice steps 1–4 during each training session. Once you can do these steps without any problems, start holding the animal a little higher and gradually increasing how long you hold him. Whenever your pet behaves calmly, click and reward.

6 When your pet is consistently being calm during step 5, raise him again at the end of the exercise and slowly turn your body to move him until he is outside the pen or over a different part of the floor than before. The first time he handles this without fidgeting, click and give a jackpot.

Tip

The Training Assistant

For this exercise, it is advantageous to have two trainers. One of you can fully concentrate on lifting the animal while the other uses the clicker and gives the rewards.

GETTING USED TO THE PET CARRIER

Suitable for: All small pets
Difficulty level: Easy to medium
Required tools: Pet carrier, clicker, treats, possibly a target stick at the beginning of the exercise

Do you have a trip to the vet coming up, and you are worried about having to transport your pet in his carrier? Is your animal terrified when he has to go into the carrier, even if only for a few minutes? Then this is the perfect exercise for you and your pet. If your small animal sees the carrier as a friendly place and not a dark, scary one, future trips will be less stressful.

If your pet gets used to being enclosed in the pet carrier, you can also take him with you when you travel. However, keep in mind that this would still be very stressful for your animal and should only be done in rare circumstances.

How it's done:

1 Guide your pet into the carrier using the target stick. You can also put him directly inside the carrier, but I prefer the target-stick method because it doesn't impose any constraints on the animal, and the animal will enter the carrier voluntarily. The prerequisite, however, is that your pet has already mastered the target stick with confidence. You do not need the target stick for the rest of this exercise.

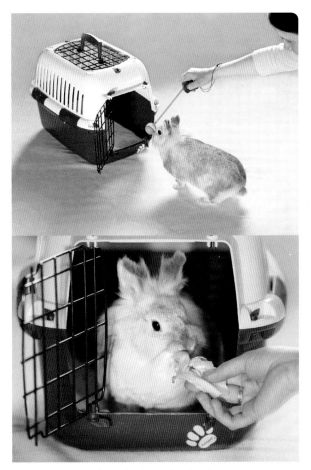

The target stick leads the animal to the carrier; he gets his reward once inside.

2 When your rodent is inside the carrier, click and reward him and allow him to exit the carrier. Repeat steps 1 and 2 several times before moving on.

3 Now your pet should begin to stay in the carrier a little longer. To do this, close the carrier briefly with your pet inside and then open it again a few seconds later. If the animal behaves

Tip

Staying Relaxed in the Car

Many animals are afraid of being in moving cars. Keep car trips as short as possible and avoid exposing your pet to heat and drafts. Sometimes turning on the radio quietly can help if the animal is used to music. With a second person as a training assistant, one of you can reinforce the animal's calm behavior with clicks and treats.

calmly in the carrier, click and reward. It is important to reward your little training partner while he is still inside the carrier.

4 Next, begin to gradually extend the time between closing and opening the carrier. Always click and reward when your pet is still in the carrier. Be sure to have good timing—watch your animal closely so that you can click and reward and open the carrier door before he shows any signs of stress or panic. Reward great progress with a jackpot.

5 Once your pet is relaxed with step 4, you can start lifting the pet carrier as soon your animal goes inside it. Initially, you should only lift the box an inch or so (3cm) off the ground and gently place it back down again right away. If your animal stays calm and relaxed, click and give a jackpot.

6 The next, and last, step is not only to lift the transport box but also to carry it and walk around with it. As usual, you should start with a short period of time

so as not to scare your pet. Reinforce calm behavior with a click and reward, or a jackpot for the first time.

GOOD BEHAVIOR IN THE CAGE

Suitable for: All small pets
Difficulty level: Medium
Tools needed: Clicker, treats

What exactly is "good behavior?" It all depends on the behavior you want from your small pet. Perhaps you would like your little darling to wait patiently while you put his food bowl in the cage. Or maybe you don't want to worry that your furry friend will try to escape and go exploring as soon as you open the cage door.

Various behavior problems can arise in everyday life with animals, and you can use clicker training for these situations. However, you should limit yourself to modifying behaviors to keep your pet out of danger rather than restricting the animal's natural behaviors. Before you start training, think carefully about whether the animal is really misbehaving or just displaying a behavior quirk specific to that animal. You cannot and should not try to get rid of the latter; it is not up to us to change an individual's character. Also consider whether the animal's undesirable behavior is due to a circumstance that you can change, such as a too-small cage, an improper cage setup, or less-than-optimal nutrition.

We will use the following example in the training steps: Every time you enter the room, your gang of guinea pigs hangs onto the bars of the cage and gnaws on them until you give them something to eat or at least pay attention to them. You may have already tried to get rid of this annoying behavior. Some recommend coating the cage bars with vinegar, but that only makes the animals uncomfortable in their pen because they dislike the smell, and they go back to their old habits anyway when the smell dissipates.

When modifying unwanted behavior, your pet receives a click and reward only if he stops showing the behavior. If he continues to show the unwanted behavior, ignore him.

How it's done:

1 When you enter the room, stop near the cage. Wait until the animals are calm. It's fine if they stand up and look at you as long as they are not gnawing on the bars of the cage. You may have to be patient for a few minutes.

2 Only when none of the animals are gnawing can you click and give each of them a treat.

3 If the animals immediately go back to gnawing on the bars because they

Only when your animals greet you without gnawing do they get their reward.

want more treats, ignore them again and wait until they have calmed down. It is helpful if you turn your back to the cage and be completely passive—do not talk or walk around.

4 Strictly adhere to this procedure every time you enter the room. You will see that the undesirable behavior occurs less and less frequently and may disappear after a while.

STRESS-FREE NAIL CLIPPING

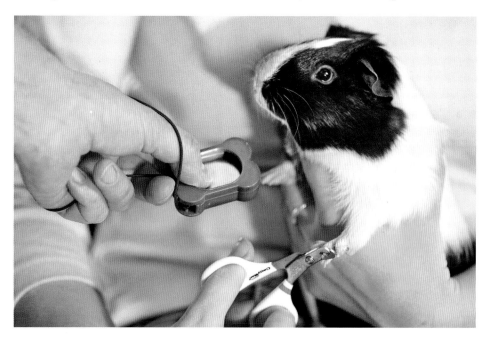

Suitable for: All small pets who do not like having their nails clipped
Difficulty level: Medium
Required tools: Nail clippers, clickers, treats, someone to act as a training assistant

The nails, or claws, of rodents and rabbits are always growing. In the wild, the claws wear down on their own as the animals dig and walk over stones or other rough surfaces. This isn't the case for household pets, even though you should try to recreate your pets' natural environment as much as possible in their pen—this includes branches, rough surfaces, and an area for digging.

Nevertheless, you should check your small pet's nails regularly. With rabbits and guinea pigs, the nails usually need to be clipped every four to six weeks. Smaller rodents, like hamsters, mice, and degus, need their nails clipped less often or, if you are lucky, not at all. Nails

Lessen the stress of nail clipping with the help of clicker training.

Clicker Training for Rabbits, Guinea Pigs, and Other Small Pets

that are too long make walking difficult and can cause painful calluses due to an incorrect gait, not to mention that the animal can get his nails caught and injure his feet.

It is best to use special nail clippers from the pet-supply shop. Always cut the nails so that they retain their natural shape: not straight across, but angled at the tips. There is a blood vessel that runs through each claw, and this is easily visible with light claws. With dark claws, you can use a flashlight to see the blood vessels better. Ideally, clip the nails to about a millimeter or two longer than the blood vessel. If you ever accidentally nick the blood vessel, press the nail into a bar of soap to stop the bleeding faster.

What can you do if your pet doesn't want to have his nails cut? What if he fidgets, scratches, and shrieks as soon as you start to get close to his feet with the nail clippers? The following steps should help remedy this problem and make it easier for you to cut his nails. You will need an assistant to hold the animal while you clip the nails and click the clicker.

How it's done:

1 Have your training assistant hold the animal with one hand around the belly and the other supporting the rear, with the animal's back against your assistant's belly. Ideally, your assistant is holding the animal's front feet between the middle and index fingers of one hand. This will

Just a Little

Tip

So that you can practice step 5 in peace, it is a good idea to shorten the nails only a tiny bit each time so that you can repeat the exercise for a few days in a row. Once your rodent understands and is comfortable with the exercise, you can clip the nails to the desired length in one sitting.

make it a little easier for you to cut your pet's nails later.

2 If your pet behaves calmly and does not wriggle around in this unfamiliar position, click, let him down, and give him a treat. Some animals also like to eat while they are being held this way, so if this is the case with your pet, your assistant doesn't have to put him down every time you click. However, if your pet struggles, wait up to a minute for him to calm down so you can click and treat. If he continues to struggle for longer than a minute, have your assistant put him down with no click. Try again later.

3 Once your assistant can hold your animal easily, take one of your pet's feet in your hand. You will need to keep his foot still while clipping his nails to avoid cutting into the blood vessel if your pet starts to fidget. If your pet allows you to hold his foot, click and reward.

4 After you have repeated step 3 several times without your pet showing signs of discomfort, you can introduce him to

the nail clippers. To do this, touch one nail with the clippers, almost as if you were going to cut the nail. If your pet doesn't flinch, click and reward.

5 The next step is to actually clip the nails. Start with just one nail and then click and reward with a jackpot immediately afterward. Continue clipping, clicking and giving a treat after each nail. You won't do this every time—later, you will click and reward only if your pet remains still and calm throughout the entire process. After a while, he will

You can safely cut your guinea pig's nails with the help of an assistant.

understand exactly when he will receive his reward.

SITTING STILL FOR GROOMING

Suitable for: All small pets who dislike being groomed
Difficulty level: Medium
Tools needed: Brush, clicker, treats

Daily grooming is a must, especially for longhaired small pets such as Angora rabbits or curly-coated animals such as Merino guinea pigs, because overgrown hair can be very bothersome to them. A short haircut is practical and more comfortable for the animal in the summer, but if you prefer keeping his coat long, you might have a problem if your otherwise trusting animal becomes scared as soon as you go near him with a brush.

With the following exercise, you can eliminate or at least greatly reduce your pet's aversion to grooming. However, you should first consider why the animal does not want you to brush him. Is it just a fear of the brush or comb? Is grooming painful due to matted hair? Or is your pet reluctant about being touched in general? If the latter is the case, you should do the Overcoming the Fear of Being Touched exercise (see page 61) with your pet before you attempt brushing him.

A soft brush is best for grooming because it won't injure your pet if he unexpectedly jumps or turns around. Combs are usually less suitable because they are not very effective for shorthaired animals and can be uncomfortable for longhaired animals. It is a good idea to use a separate brush for each of your pets because the smell of another animal on the brush could make an animal uncomfortable or distract him so much that he cannot enjoy the grooming experience. Carefully cut out any matted areas in the fur before brushing to make grooming more comfortable and to prevent parasites from nesting in the matted fur.

How it's done:

1 It is best to sit your small pet on your lap or on the floor in front of you for this exercise. If possible, incorporate the daily grooming into your regular petting and handling so the animal gets used to it.

2 Show the brush to your pet and let him sniff it.

3 Now pet your animal on the part of his body that you want to brush first. If he stays still when you touch him, click and reward.

4 Run the smooth back of the brush over the same area of your pet's body. If he stays calm, click and reward.

5 Gently and quickly run the bristles of the brush over this area of fur. This step should create a positive basis for further grooming. If your pet remains calm, click and reward.

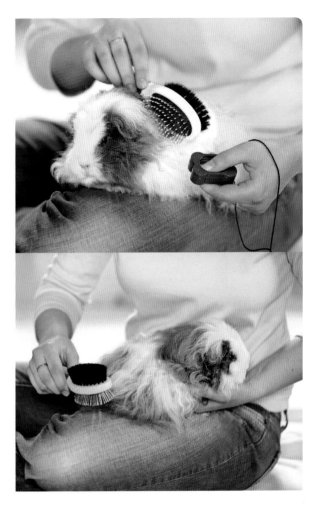

Guinea pig Ida enjoys being groomed.
Always use a soft brush, brushing in short intervals until the animal gets used to it.

6 Once your pet consistently stays calm when you do step 5, you can start to brush with a little more pressure, but only as much as your animal is comfortable with. Click and reward him for staying calm.

No Tugging

Use a very soft brush that won't tug on the animal's fur.

7 Gradually start grooming the rest of the animal. For sensitive parts of his body, such as the face or stomach, either be particularly careful or don't use the brush at all in these areas. If your pet stays calm, click and reward. The first time he stays calm for a longer brushing session, rewarded him with a jackpot.

NO UNWANTED CHEWING

Does this sound familiar to you? Your rabbits, guinea pigs, or rats are running around the room, and you are sitting on the couch, reading a magazine and occasionally checking on them. Then, one of the animals disappears under a desk. You stand up, rush over to the desk, and stop him just as he was about to start nibbling on your computer cords. It could have been a very bad situation if you hadn't gotten there in time.

Wouldn't it be nice if you could use your clicker to stop your pets from nibbling on electrical cords and other forbidden objects? In theory, you can.

This is another exercise that trains a passive behavior. If you have practiced Good Behavior in the Cage (see page 78), you know that you click only when your pets are calm and not gnawing on the bars. If the animals show undesirable behavior, you ignore them and wait to click until you see the desired behavior again. Teaching your pets not to chew on household objects is based on the same principle; however, there's a problem with this: you cannot wait for an animal to stop chewing because if he gnaws all the way through an electrical cord, he could suffer a fatal electric shock.

There are limitations to clicker training, and this exercise shows one of those limitations. You will not find specific step-by-step clicker instructions here because it is very difficult and not successful for every animal. With enough training, your small pet can learn that chewing on wires is unacceptable behavior, but there is no guarantee that your animal will not relapse when you're not watching. But there are ways to protect your little nibblers.

1 Make it impossible for your small pets to access cords and cables. You can "chew-proof" your room with just a little effort by running cables behind baseboards or using cord protectors. If you want to prevent your animals from crawling under or behind furniture, block off these areas with pillows or blankets. Along with these precautions, never leave your pet in a danger zone without supervision, even if he usually does not engage in potentially harmful behavior.

2 The need for small animals, such as rabbits, guinea pigs, hamsters, and the like, to gnaw on things is natural and cannot be suppressed, so you shouldn't

A rabbit-safe tree, such as hazelnut, gives your rabbits branches to nibble on whenever the urge strikes.

try to stop the behavior altogether. The word *rodent* comes from a Latin word meaning "to gnaw," and this applies to rabbits as well. Gnawing is important for these animals because their teeth never stop growing. By chewing on branches and hay, they wear their teeth down and maintain them at a proper size. Always give your pets enough safe items to gnaw on so that they do not have to look elsewhere to get their fix.

3 If one of your pets tries to nibble on electrical cords when he is running around the room freely, immediately end playtime by putting the animal back in his cage and ignoring him.

4 Here's a clicker tip: Place several branches in your pet's free-running space. If he nibbles on them, reinforce the behavior with a click and a reward. If he doesn't go to these "chew toys" on his own, you can use the target stick to guide him.

CHAPTER 7

Click According to Plan

>>
Progress doesn't happen
overnight! Recording your
pet's training improvements
can put into perspective
how clicker exercises
can transform him from
beginner to hurdle-jumper.

Twenty-Five Days of Clicks

Keeping a training diary is very useful and helps you better understand the exercises and how your pet progresses with each of them. The following example is from one of my own training diaries.

Day 1

Today I started clicker training with guinea pig Oliver. Although Oliver has been living with me for a few weeks, he is still a little suspicious and shy around people. I hope that we can reduce this behavior with the help of clicker training.

Oliver's big day: the first clicker session.

First, I let Oliver explore the new training location in peace and quiet. I decided on the kitchen as a neutral training place because it doesn't smell like my other animals, and the little guinea pig doesn't get distracted there. I put his blue blanket on the floor to help put him at ease in this new environment. Our training sessions will always take place on this blanket.

After Oliver finished examining his new surroundings, I clicked the clicker and immediately gave him a treat: a small piece of lettuce. At first, he found the clicking sound a bit confusing, but after I clicked and rewarded him a few times, he got used to it. Because I use a clicker with adjustable volume during training, I set it to the quietest level, which made it easier for Oliver to get used to the sound.

After about fifteen clicks and treats, I finished our first session and put the guinea pig back in the pen with his friends.

Day 2

Oliver was very excited when I put him on his cozy blanket (which is now his training blanket) in the kitchen. He ran back and forth curiously and had to sniff everything very carefully. He didn't leave the blanket because the floor is tiled and therefore smooth and cold. I was happy about that because it would make training difficult if Oliver wanted to crawl around under the dining table and chairs—and I had to chase after him!

Today I just clicked and immediately gave Oliver his rewards. Remarkably, he got used to the clicking sound quickly. Although the sound is relatively loud to guinea pig ears, he acted as if it were perfectly normal.

Day 3

The third session was also about conditioning the clicker. I would have loved to start training with the target stick, but if the animal doesn't yet fully understand the connection between the click and the reward, any further training would be useless. For this reason, I had to be patient today and continue to delight Oliver with many little veggie treats, which he basically received for doing nothing.

Day 4

Today I repeated clicker conditioning a few times at the beginning of our training session and then started target-stick training. I held the target stick right in front of little Oliver's nose, and, when he sniffed it curiously, I clicked and rewarded him. The exercise went quite well a few times, but then Oliver lost interest in the new game and decided to start running around the blanket.

When he came near me again, I put the target stick in front of his nose again, and, lo and behold, he actually sniffed it and got his click and treat. However,

I am not sure if he really understands that I only click when he touches the ball on the target stick. He is probably just intrigued by this strange thing that I keep waving in his face, and that's why he nudges it. But I'm sure he will soon understand the connection between the clicker sound and his behavior. Oliver and I ended the training session after about twenty minutes.

Day 5

Unfortunately, we made no progress today. Oliver and I practiced again with the target stick, but we ended the training session after a short time. My training partner was very distracted today and was interested in everything but the target stick. Oh, well! Guinea pigs can also have bad days.

Day 6

What Oliver lacked yesterday, he more than made up for in today's training. I was able to hold the target stick a little farther away, and he still stretched for it. He also has no problem turning his head to the side to touch the ball of the target stick. He is clearly a very teachable animal and is enjoying training more and more. I'm really excited to see how our training sessions will progress.

Day 10

I took a break from writing over the last few days—but not a break from training. I have some more progress to report: Oliver has now learned to follow the target stick for a few steps. He does this so well, and it is a pleasure to watch. You can now clearly see that he enjoys training just as much as I do. However, it is also apparent that our training sessions are quite exhausting for Oliver, so I decided to stop training twice a day for a few days.

Day 12

Oliver is following the target stick for longer and longer distances. Sometimes he gets distracted by other things and stops halfway, but most of the time I can bring his attention back to clicker training right away. Recently, when I tap the target stick on the floor lightly, Oliver comes running eagerly to find the source of the noise.

Oliver no longer takes his eyes off the target stick.

Day 15

Today I started teaching Oliver to stand up on his hind legs. He is also quite happy to stretch his nose up so that he can touch the ball on the target stick. It is not yet clear to him, though, that he should stand on his hind legs to do this. If I hold the target stick at a height that he can only reach by standing up, he simply walks away and looks for something else to do. I probably just need to give him some more time. You really can't expect a pet to learn a whole new trick in a single day.

Day 25

Oliver's repertoire of tricks now includes very confident target training, standing up on his hind legs without any help, and following the target stick over a bridge (admittedly, a very flat bridge!).

Clicker Training for Rabbits, Guinea Pigs, and Other Small Pets

Today I wanted to show Oliver's progress to a friend, and I started training as usual: first, a warm-up with very simple targeting and no long distances. But the little guinea pig just sat there without moving and looked at the target stick with his big button eyes. I thought he had been acting a bit sluggish today, so I tried to cheer him on, but my friend didn't get to see much more than a little targeting—which understandably led to some sarcastic remarks about my "great clicker performer."

Obviously, Oliver is not ready to give demonstrations in front of an audience yet. Even though our spectator was calm, Oliver was distracted and had to keep sniffing her. The little guinea pig also definitely felt some tension from me because I wanted to show off his tricks. We will have to train a lot before our next performance because we're still far from clicker greatness!

The playful training sessions with Oliver are more and more fun each day, so I'm ending this diary entry knowing that we will have more success moving forward despite one failed attempt at a demonstration.

Standing up on his hind legs is one of Oliver's favorite exercises.

HOW TO RECORD YOUR RESULTS

If you want to try out clicker training with several animals, it is helpful to document each one's training results. This way, you can compare each animal's progress and see how quickly each one masters each exercise. This makes training much easier in the future because you can use your results with one animal as a sort of training plan—or at least a guideline—for another. This can be particularly helpful when training different animals of the same species, keeping in mind that each individual pet will be a little different.

Training Log

Pet's name: ....

Species and breed: ....

Age: .... Has lived with me since: ....

Special characteristics: ....

Training goal: ....

Training session #	Duration of training session:
What did we work on?	
Progress:	
Notes:	

Training session #	Duration of training session:
What did we work on?	
Progress:	
Notes:	

Training session #	Duration of training session:
What did we work on?	
Progress:	
Notes:	

Training session #	Duration of training session:

What did we work on?

Progress:

Notes:

Training session #	Duration of training session:

What did we work on?

Progress:

Notes:

Training session #	Duration of training session:

What did we work on?

Progress:

Notes:

Training session #	Duration of training session:

What did we work on?

Progress:

Notes:

Clicker Training For Rabbits, Guinea Pigs, and Other Small Pets © 2023 CompanionHouse Books

More Great CompanionHouse Books

Chinchillas
A Guide to Caring for
Your Chinchilla
Donna Anastasi
Paperback
160 pages • 5½" x 8½"
978-1-93395-815-6

Guinea Pigs
Practical Advice to Caring
for Your Guinea Pig
Virgina Parker Guidry
Paperback
144 pages • 5½" x 8½"
978-1-93199-332-6

Hamsters
The Ultimate Pocket Pet
Virgina Parker Guidry
Paperback
120 pages • 5½" x 8½"
978-1-93199-331-9

Rabbits
Small-Scale Rabbit Keeping
Christine McLaughlin
Paperback
160 pages • 6" x 9"
978-1-93395-896-5

Rat Training
The Comprehensive
Beginner's Guide
Miriam Fields-Babineau
Paperback
160 pages • 5½" x 8½"
978-1-93395-868-2

Rats
Practical Advice
from the Expert
Debbie Ducommun
Paperback
176 pages • 5½" x 8½"
978-1-93548-464-6

Index

Acknowledgments

Thank you to Florina Strobel, Eisenach; Carla Cronauer, Baden-Baden; Jasmin Berg, Herleshausen; and Dieko Chinahandel GmbH, Schneverdingen (www.strohteppich.de) for their help and support with the photo shoots for this book.

Photo Credits

All interior and back cover photos by Regina Kuhn, Herleshausen
Shutterstock.com anetapics, front cover; photobac, page 34
Illustrations by Shutterstock.com and Vecteasy.com

About the Author

Veterinarian Isabel Müller has been successfully training her own rabbits, guinea pigs, cats, and budgerigars with the clicker for many years. Her small pets have demonstrated their skills on television.